To:

....

From:

....

Date:

....

A Faith-Filled,
Family Favorite Holiday Cookbook

Christmas
DELIGHTS

BARBOUR BOOKS
An Imprint of Barbour Publishing, Inc.

ISBN 978-1-64352-545-7

Compiled by Debbie Cole.

Published by Barbour Books, an imprint of Barbour Publishing, Inc., 1810 Barbour Drive, Uhrichsville, Ohio, 44683, www.barbourbooks.com.

Our mission is to inspire the world with the life-changing message of the Bible.

Member of the
Evangelical Christian
Publishers Association

Printed in China.

CONTENTS

7

Refreshing Beverages

21

Bountiful Breakfasts and Brunches

67

Christmas Dinner, including Main Dishes and Sides

113

Christmas Eve Celebrations

125

Cookies and Candy

173

Festive Breads

195

Merrymaking: Party Dishes to Feed a Crowd

It's the most *delightful* time of the year. . . .

The Christmas season is a time for visiting with family and friends, reaching out to strangers, celebrating traditions, and making memories. It's also a time when food becomes more than food—even common recipes take on a magical quality. The recipes in this book were chosen because they warm and inspire. They are easy to make and easy to share. We hope you will see the magic in each and every one as you move tastefully through your holiday season!

Father God, as we celebrate Christmas with all the joyful traditions that make this time of year so special, may we also give praise for the gift of Your Son, Jesus, who was born to redeem us. Amen.

Refreshing
BEVERAGES

Christmas. . .is not an external event at all,
but a piece of one's home that one carries in one's heart.
FREYA STARK

Lord, our souls are parched and longing for You!
As the deer pants after the refreshment of the
stream, lead us each day to quench our thirst with
the pure living water of Your Word. Amen.

Whether you eat or drink or
whatever you do, do it all
for the glory of God.
1 Corinthians 10:31 niv

Choco-Mint Cocoa

½ cup sugar
¼ cup instant cocoa mix
3 ounces dark chocolate chips
⅓ cup hot water
4 cups milk

1 teaspoon vanilla
¼ teaspoon peppermint extract
4 large peppermint candy canes,
   crushed

Mix sugar, cocoa mix, chocolate chips, and hot water in saucepan over medium heat, stirring continually until chocolate chips are melted. Add milk, vanilla, and peppermint extract. Stir until well blended and hot. Serve in mugs with a sprinkling of crushed candy cane. YIELD: 1½ QUARTS.

Cinnamon Cocoa

4 cups whole milk
1 cup chocolate syrup
1 teaspoon cinnamon

1 cup whipping cream, whipped
¼ cup semisweet mini
   chocolate chips

Heat together milk and syrup in saucepan. Stir in cinnamon and serve in mugs. Garnish with whipped cream and chocolate chips. YIELD: 5 TO 6 CUPS.

Cranberry Apple Sippers

2 cups cranapple juice cocktail
½ cup whole milk
½ cup half-and-half

½ teaspoon nutmeg
¼ cup sugar
1 cup crushed ice

Put all ingredients in blender and blend until smooth. YIELD: 3 CUPS.

Cranberry Spritzers

1 quart cranberry juice cocktail
2½ tablespoons lemon juice
Ginger ale

Mix together first two ingredients. Fill serving glasses half full. Add cold ginger ale to fill each glass and stir gently. Yield: 4 servings.

Down Under Christmas Smoothies

8 very ripe kiwi
2 teaspoons lime juice
½ cup raspberry drinking yogurt

1 cup lemonade
12 ounces cream soda or ginger ale

Peel kiwis and puree in blender with lime juice until smooth. Add yogurt and lemonade. Mix with sparkling soda to serve. YIELD: 3 TO 4 SERVINGS.

Eggnog

½ cup sugar
3 egg yolks, beaten
¼ teaspoon salt
4 cups scalded milk

½ teaspoon vanilla
3 egg whites
¼ cup sugar
¼ teaspoon nutmeg

Beat ½ cup sugar, egg yolks, and salt until lemon colored. Gradually pour milk into egg mixture; chill. Add vanilla. When ready to serve, make meringue of egg whites and ¼ cup sugar. Fold into chilled mixture. Sprinkle with nutmeg.

French Chocolate

1 cup semisweet chocolate chips
½ cup light corn syrup
¼ cup water

1 teaspoon vanilla
1 pint heavy cream
1 quart whole milk

Mix all ingredients in large saucepan and heat slowly, stirring constantly until chocolate chips are melted. A very rich chocolate drink to be served warm. YIELD: 8 TO 10 CUPS.

Hot Chai

2 cups water
4 tea bags black tea
4 tablespoons honey
½ teaspoon vanilla
½ teaspoon cinnamon

4 cloves
¼ teaspoon cardamom
¼ teaspoon ginger
1 pinch nutmeg
2 cups milk

Bring water to boil; add next 8 ingredients. Simmer for 5 minutes. Add milk; boil. Remove from heat and strain liquid before serving. YIELD: 4 CUPS.

Hot Chocolate

3 cups milk
⅓ cup grated semisweet chocolate
1 tablespoon sugar

Heat milk in microwave-safe bowl. Add grated chocolate and sugar and stir until dissolved. YIELD: 3 CUPS.

Hot Spiced Tea

6 cups water
1 teaspoon whole cloves
1 cinnamon stick
2 tablespoons loose black tea

1 cup orange juice
2 tablespoons lemon juice
¾ cup sugar

Combine water, cloves, and cinnamon stick in saucepan. Bring to a boil and remove from heat. Add tea, stir, and cover. While tea steeps for 5 minutes, bring juices and sugar just to a boil. Stir into hot tea and strain into cups. YIELD: 6 CUPS.

Mint-Chocolate Coffee Mix

¼ cup instant coffee granules

¼ cup powdered nondairy
    coffee creamer

⅓ cup sugar

2 tablespoons cocoa

1½ tablespoons crushed
    hard peppermint candies

Place all ingredients in blender and process until well blended. Yield: 8 servings.

As a Gift: Present the coffee mix in a glass jar. Add a label with these serving directions: *Combine 2 tablespoons Mint-Chocolate Coffee Mix and ¾ cup boiling water; stir well.*

Mulled Cider Mix

2 cups sweetened instant cider mix
1 teaspoon cinnamon

½ teaspoon ground cloves
¼ teaspoon salt

Mix together cider mix, spices, and salt. YIELD: ABOUT 16 SERVINGS.

As a Gift: Present the cider mix in a decorative tin or glass jar. Make a greeting tag and tie it to the neck of the container with raffia. Include this serving suggestion: *Add 2 tablespoons cider mix to 1 cup boiling water; stir well.*

Peppermint Cocoa Mix

16 ounces nondairy creamer
8 cups nonfat dry milk
1 pound powdered sugar

3 tablespoons dark cocoa
Dash salt
1 cup crushed candy cane

Mix together creamer, milk, sugar, cocoa, salt, and crushed candy canes. Store in lidded container. YIELD: ABOUT 12 CUPS.

As a Gift: Present the cocoa mix in a decorative lidded tin. Tie a ribbon to the top of the tin and attach a label and a bundle of tiny candy canes. Include this serving suggestion: *Add ⅓ cup cocoa mix to 1 cup hot water; stir well.*

Peppermint Mocha Soda

Chocolate syrup
Club soda or ginger ale, chilled
Peppermint stick ice cream

Whipped cream
Maraschino cherries

For each soda, place 3 tablespoons chocolate syrup in tall glass. Fill glass half full with chilled club soda or ginger ale. Add 2 scoops ice cream and stir gently. Garnish with whipped cream and cherry.

Pineapple Frost

2 cups pineapple juice
1 pint vanilla ice cream
2 tablespoons lemon juice

Put all ingredients in blender and blend until smooth. Yield: 4 servings.

Pineapple-Orange Fizzes

3 cups orange juice
1 (8 ounce) can crushed pineapple, with juice

1 glass crushed ice
Ginger ale, chilled

Blend first three ingredients until smooth. Fill serving glasses half full. Add chilled ginger ale to fill each glass. Stir gently and serve. Yield: 6 servings.

Raspberry Lemonade

2 (12 ounce) cans frozen lemonade concentrate, thawed
2 (10 ounce) packages frozen sweetened raspberries, partially thawed

4 tablespoons sugar
2 liters club soda, chilled
Ice cubes

Mix lemonade concentrate, raspberries, and sugar in blender. Strain to remove seeds. Combine raspberry mixture with club soda; add ice cubes and mix well. Serve immediately.

Pumpkin Nog

1 (29 ounce) can pumpkin puree
1 pint vanilla ice cream, softened
4 cups milk
1 teaspoon cinnamon

½ teaspoon nutmeg
¼ teaspoon ginger
1 cup whipped topping

Load a blender with small portions of pumpkin, ice cream, milk, and spices; blend thoroughly. Transfer blended ingredients to large pitcher and pour into mugs. Garnish with whipped topping and a sprinkle of cinnamon if desired. Yield: 10 servings.

Yuletide Chocolate Lover's Coffee

4 (1 ounce) squares semisweet
   chocolate, chopped
2 cups half-and-half

4 cups hot brewed coffee
¾ cup coffee liqueur
Sweetened whipped topping

In large saucepan, combine chocolate and half-and-half over medium-low heat. Whisk constantly for 10 minutes or until chocolate is melted and smooth. Stir in coffee. Remove from heat and stir in liqueur. Serve warm with whipped topping. YIELD: 8 SERVINGS.

Rich "South of the Border" Hot Chocolate

9 cups milk
½ cup packed dark brown sugar
2 (3.5 ounce) chocolate candy bars
⅓ cup dutch-process or unsweetened cocoa powder
3 tablespoons instant espresso powder
1½ teaspoons cinnamon
⅔ cup coffee liqueur (optional)
Sweetened whipped cream and cinnamon or vanilla beans for garnish

Heat milk, dark brown sugar, candy bars, cocoa, espresso powder, and cinnamon in dutch oven over medium heat for 10 minutes or until chocolate melts and sugar dissolves, stirring occasionally. Remove from heat and whisk vigorously until hot chocolate is frothy. Immediately pour into mugs. Stir a splash of coffee liqueur into each serving if desired. Top with whipped cream and sprinkle with cinnamon or add a vanilla bean to each mug as a stir stick. YIELD: 11 SERVINGS.

Vanilla Ginger Latte

1 teaspoon ginger syrup
2 ounces espresso
¼ teaspoon vanilla
¾ cup steaming milk

Pour ginger syrup into mug; add espresso and stir. Add vanilla, then milk, and serve.

Spicy Grape Punch

2 cups grape juice
½ cup sugar
1 cinnamon stick
1 teaspoon whole cloves
1 tablespoon lemon juice
1 (6 ounce) can frozen orange juice
   concentrate, thawed
1 cup water

Combine all ingredients in large saucepan and bring to a boil. Remove cinnamon stick and cloves and serve hot. YIELD: 8 SERVINGS.

Spicy Tea

18 ounces orange drink mix
2¼ cups sugar
2 teaspoons cinnamon
1 cup instant tea mix
1 teaspoon ground cloves
1 (4.6 ounce) package powdered
   lemonade

Mix all ingredients and place in airtight jar. To serve, add 2 to 3 teaspoons tea mix to 1 cup boiling water; stir well.

Bountiful
BREAKFASTS
and BRUNCHES

Christmas is not a time nor a season, but a state of mind.
To cherish peace and goodwill, to be plenteous in mercy,
is to have the real spirit of Christmas.
CALVIN COOLIDGE

Father in heaven, every beautiful day begins
with You! Remind us each morning that as we
rested You were watching over us, never sleeping,
ever attentive. Fill our waking hearts
with grateful prayer. Amen.

*[The virtuous woman] gets up
before dawn to prepare breakfast
for her household.*

Proverbs 31:15 NLT

Breakfast

Apple Pancake Pie

½ cup plus 2 tablespoons flour
½ cup plus 2 tablespoons milk
4 eggs
5 tablespoons butter or margarine

1 red apple, cut into slices
    with skin on
2 tablespoons sugar
Powdered sugar

Mix flour, milk, and eggs until slightly lumpy. Melt butter in 10-inch pie pan in oven until hot and bubbly. Pour batter over hot butter in pie pan. Roll apple slices in sugar and place pinwheel fashion in center of batter. Bake at 450 degrees for 25 to 30 minutes or until sides of pancake rise above center and brown. Remove from oven and sprinkle with powdered sugar. Serve immediately with syrup.

Apple Pancakes

2 eggs
2 cups flour, sifted
1 cup milk
1 cup applesauce

1 teaspoon salt
2 tablespoons baking powder
4 tablespoons butter, melted

In large bowl, combine all ingredients, mixing until smooth. Drop scoops of batter onto hot griddle or into skillet and fry until golden brown. Serve warm with syrup. YIELD: ABOUT 16 PANCAKES.

Bacon Gravy

2 to 4 slices bacon, cut into
  small pieces
⅓ cup flour
½ teaspoon salt

⅛ teaspoon black pepper
1 teaspoon sugar
3 cups milk

Fry bacon pieces over medium heat until crisp. Stir in flour until grease is absorbed. Season with salt, pepper, and sugar. Slowly whisk in milk, stirring until mixture reaches a boil. Boil for 5 minutes or until thick. Serve over biscuits, toast, or potatoes.

Blueberry Coffee Cake

CAKE:
¾ cup sugar
¼ cup butter
1 egg
½ cup milk
2 cups flour
2 teaspoons baking powder
½ teaspoon salt
2 cups blueberries, partially frozen

TOPPING:
1 cup sugar
⅔ cup flour
½ cup butter
1 teaspoon cinnamon

In large bowl, mix cake ingredients. Pour batter into greased and floured 9x13-inch pan; set aside. In separate bowl, mix topping ingredients and sprinkle topping over cake batter. Bake at 350 degrees for 35 to 40 minutes.

Blueberry Pancakes

2 cups flour
2 teaspoons baking powder
½ teaspoon salt
1 egg, beaten
⅓ cup vegetable oil
1 cup buttermilk
1 tablespoon butter
1 cup blueberries

Blend dry ingredients. Stir in egg, oil, and buttermilk. If batter is too thick, add a little water or regular milk to make good pancake consistency. Melt butter in skillet or on flat griddle. When very hot, pour two to three pancakes at a time, dotting with several blueberries. As air bubbles dot surface of batter, flip pancakes and cook about 1 minute longer. YIELD: 15 PANCAKES.

Breakfast Casserole

6 to 8 slices bread, torn into
    small pieces
1 pound sausage, cooked
    and crumbled
1 cup shredded cheddar cheese

6 to 8 eggs
2 cups milk
1 teaspoon mustard
¼ teaspoon salt

Grease 9x13-inch pan and place bread pieces in bottom. Sprinkle sausage and cheese over bread. In large bowl, beat eggs and milk until fluffy; add mustard and salt. Pour over bread, sausage, and cheese. Casserole may be refrigerated overnight. Bake at 350 degrees for 45 minutes.

Breakfast Pizza

1 tube refrigerated pizza crust
1 pound cubed ham
1 cup chopped onion
1 teaspoon butter
6 eggs
2 tablespoons heavy cream

16 ounces fresh salsa
½ teaspoon salt
½ teaspoon pepper
1½ cups shredded Mexican-style
    cheese

Unroll pizza crust dough and press into lightly greased pizza pan. Bake at 400 degrees for 8 minutes. While crust cools, brown ham and onions together in butter. Drain and set aside. Clean pan and lightly oil it. In mixing bowl, beat eggs and mix in cream. Pour into pan and scramble. Spread salsa on partially cooked pizza crust and top with ham, onions, and scrambled eggs. Sprinkle with salt, pepper, and shredded cheese. Return to oven and bake 10 to 12 minutes longer or until crust is golden brown and cheese is bubbly. YIELD: 8 SMALL SLICES.

Buttermilk Pancakes

2 cups sifted flour
1 teaspoon soda
1 teaspoon salt
2 tablespoons sugar

2 eggs, beaten
2 cups buttermilk
2 tablespoons oil
1 teaspoon vanilla

In large bowl, combine dry ingredients. Add remaining ingredients and stir just until moistened. Drop scoops of batter onto hot griddle or into skillet and fry until golden brown. Serve warm with syrup.

Chorizo and Egg Burritos

4 flour tortillas
1 pound chorizo sausage
½ cup chopped onion
4 eggs
½ teaspoon salt

½ teaspoon pepper
2 cups shredded Mexican-style cheese
Salsa and sour cream

Roll each tortilla in damp paper towel and place in warm (250 degrees) oven. Brown sausage and onion together. In separate pan, scramble eggs with salt and pepper. Unroll warm tortillas and fill with sausage, eggs, and cheese. Roll up, place in baking dish, and return to oven for 10 minutes. Serve garnished with salsa and sour cream. YIELD: 4 SERVINGS.

Caramel Apple Grits

1 cup heavy cream
2 cups whole milk
1 teaspoon cinnamon
1 teaspoon salt
½ teaspoon vanilla
3 tablespoons brown sugar

¾ cup uncooked grits
3 Granny Smith apples, peeled and
  sliced just before serving
Butter and brown sugar
¼ cup caramel syrup

Lightly oil six 1-cup ramekins (small baking dishes) and set aside. In heavy saucepan, stir together cream, milk, cinnamon, salt, vanilla, and 3 tablespoons brown sugar. Bring to a boil and stir in grits. Cook over low heat, stirring frequently, for 25 minutes or until thick and creamy. Spoon into ramekins, smoothing tops with spoon. Cover with plastic wrap and refrigerate overnight. Before serving, sauté apples with butter and brown sugar until tender. Warm grits in microwave until heated through. Warm caramel syrup for 45 seconds. Unmold warm grits onto plates and top with syrup and apples.

Yield: 6 servings.

Cheesy Grits Casserole

1 cup quick-cooking hominy grits
3 cups milk
1 teaspoon salt
¼ teaspoon pepper
2 eggs, beaten

1 cup water
6 tablespoons butter
1 cup shredded cheddar or Monterey Jack cheese
1 small can chopped green chilies

In large saucepan, combine grits, milk, salt, and pepper and cook over medium heat, stirring often to prevent scorching. When thick, remove from heat and add eggs and water until well blended. Return to burner and cook until thick again, stirring constantly. Mix in butter, cheese, and chilies. Spread in greased 9x12 inch casserole dish and bake at 325 degrees for 30 minutes.

Yield: 6 servings.

Cinnamon Coffee Cake

1½ cups flour
½ cup sugar
2½ teaspoons baking powder
½ teaspoon salt
¼ cup vegetable oil
1 egg

¾ cup milk
½ cup brown sugar
2 tablespoons flour
2 tablespoons vegetable oil
2 teaspoons cinnamon

In mixing bowl, sift together flour, sugar, baking powder, and salt. In separate bowl, combine ¼ cup oil, egg, and milk; blend into dry mixture to make batter. In another bowl, combine brown sugar, 2 tablespoons flour, 2 tablespoons oil, and cinnamon. Pour half of batter in greased 8x8-inch pan. Top with half of cinnamon-sugar mixture. Add remaining batter and top with remaining cinnamon-sugar mixture. Bake at 350 degrees for 20 to 25 minutes.

Coffee Break Cake

CAKE:
½ cup butter or margarine
1 cup sugar
1 tablespoon brown sugar
1 egg
2 cups flour
½ teaspoon salt
2 teaspoons baking powder

¾ cup milk
1 teaspoon vanilla
¼ teaspoon almond extract

TOPPING:
½ cup sugar
2 tablespoons butter, melted
1½ teaspoons cinnamon

In large bowl, combine all cake ingredients in order given. Pour batter into greased 7x11-inch pan; set aside. In small bowl, mix topping ingredients until crumbly; sprinkle over batter. Bake at 400 degrees for 25 minutes.

Cinnamon Raisin French Toast

6 eggs
½ cup heavy cream
1 teaspoon cinnamon
½ teaspoon salt

1 tablespoon butter
1 loaf unsliced raisin bread
Powdered sugar and whipped cream
or syrup for garnish

Beat together eggs and cream just until well blended. Add cinnamon and salt. Melt butter in skillet. While heating, cut raisin bread into 2-inch slices. Dip each slice completely into egg mixture for a few seconds. Place in hot butter and brown on first side before flipping and browning top side. Sprinkle with powdered sugar and serve with whipped cream or syrup. YIELD: 6 SERVINGS.

Cinnamon-Topped Oatmeal Muffins

1 cup flour
¼ cup sugar
3 teaspoons baking powder
½ teaspoon salt
1 cup quick-cooking oats
½ cup raisins
3 tablespoons vegetable oil
1 egg, beaten
1 cup milk

TOPPING:
2 tablespoons sugar
2 teaspoons flour
1 teaspoon cinnamon
1 teaspoon melted butter

Preheat oven to 425 degrees. In mixing bowl, sift together flour, sugar, baking powder, and salt. Stir in oats, raisins, oil, egg, and milk. Stir just until dry ingredients are moistened. Fill greased muffin cups two-thirds full; set aside. In small bowl, combine all topping ingredients and sprinkle over each muffin. Bake for 15 minutes.

Cornmeal Mush

2¾ cups water
1 cup yellow cornmeal
1 cup cold water

1 teaspoon salt
1 teaspoon sugar

In large saucepan, bring water to a boil. In small bowl, combine remaining ingredients and add to boiling water, stirring constantly. Cook over medium heat until mixture is thick, stirring frequently. Cover pan and continue cooking for 10 to 15 minutes over low heat. At this point, you may serve the hot mush with a topping of fried sausage and onions and a bit of butter if desired. Otherwise, pour hot mush into lightly greased loaf pan and chill for several hours. Turn out of pan and cut into ½-inch slices. Deep fry in oil until golden brown. Serve with butter and syrup.

Country Christmas Breakfast Casserole

½ pound spicy bulk pork sausage
½ cup finely chopped onion
4 cups diced hash brown potatoes
1½ cups shredded Colby
  Jack cheese

3 eggs, beaten
1 cup milk
¼ teaspoon pepper
Salsa

In large skillet, brown sausage and onion; drain. In 8x8-inch baking dish, layer potatoes, half of cheese, sausage mixture, and remaining cheese. In small bowl, combine eggs, milk, and pepper; pour over cheese layer. Bake uncovered at 350 degrees for 50 to 55 minutes or until knife inserted near center comes out clean. Let stand for 10 minutes before serving. Slice into squares and serve with salsa.

Creamed Eggs and Biscuits

6 tablespoons butter
6 tablespoons flour
1½ teaspoons salt
Dash pepper

3 cups milk
6 hard-boiled eggs, chopped
Ham or bacon, chopped

In saucepan, melt butter over low heat; stir in flour, salt, and pepper until well blended. Slowly add milk and stir constantly. Cook until smooth. Add eggs and ham. Serve over toast or biscuits. YIELD: 6 SERVINGS.

Deluxe Grits

4 cups water
1 cup old-fashioned grits
¼ cup butter
1 teaspoon salt

2 cups shredded cheddar cheese
6 to 8 slices bacon
4 eggs
1 cup milk

In 3-quart saucepan, bring water, grits, butter, and salt to a boil. Reduce heat to simmer for 10 minutes. Stir in cheese until melted. Allow grits to continue to simmer while frying bacon in skillet until crisp. Drain bacon on paper towel, then crumble into grits. In small bowl, beat eggs with milk. Remove grits from heat and stir in egg mixture. Pour into well-greased 9x13-inch pan. Bake at 350 degrees for 20 to 30 minutes. YIELD: 8 SERVINGS.

Crepes

3 eggs
1 cup milk
¾ cup flour
1 tablespoon sugar
½ teaspoon salt

3 to 4 tablespoons butter
Sweetened diced fruit
Whipped cream or syrup
 for garnish

Beat together eggs and milk. Stir in flour, sugar, and salt. For each crepe, melt 1 tablespoon butter in 8-inch skillet. When hot, pour 2 tablespoons batter into pan and tilt, spreading out batter to coat inside of pan. Flip to quickly cook other side. Turn out onto serving plate, fill with desired fruit, and roll up. Top with whipped cream or syrup. YIELD: 3 TO 4 CREPES.

Doughnuts

1 cup sugar

3 eggs

1 cup milk

2 tablespoons butter, melted

½ teaspoon vanilla

1 cup flour

3 teaspoons baking powder

1 teaspoon salt

¼ teaspoon nutmeg

Flour

Hot oil

Sugar, granulated or powdered (optional)

In large bowl, beat first 9 ingredients in order given. Add enough flour to make a dough that can be handled but is not too stiff. Roll out and cut into small rounds. Fry in hot oil. Eat plain or sugared.

Egg Fajitas

2 tablespoons vegetable oil
2 cups frozen hash browns
½ pound spicy bulk pork sausage
5 eggs

½ cup chopped green bell pepper
¼ cup chopped onion
8 large flour tortillas
1 cup shredded cheddar cheese

Heat oil in large skillet. Add hash browns and cook over medium heat, stirring constantly until lightly browned. Add sausage and stir frequently until sausage is thoroughly cooked. Beat eggs in small bowl and add to hash brown mixture along with green pepper and onion. Cook, stirring occasionally, until eggs are set and thoroughly cooked. Microwave tortillas on high for 25 to 30 seconds to soften. Spoon egg mixture onto center of softened tortillas and top with cheese. Roll up tortillas before serving.

Eggs Florentine

3 thin baguette slices
1 (10 ounce) package frozen
   chopped spinach, thawed
½ teaspoon pepper

3 eggs
1 teaspoon salt
3 ounces grated parmesan cheese

Preheat oven to 350 degrees. Place 1 baguette slice in bottom of each individual baking dish. Squeeze excess moisture from spinach until almost dry. Divide among each dish on top of baguette. Carefully break egg over spinach and sprinkle with salt, pepper, and parmesan. Bake for about 15 minutes or until egg whites are firm. Serve immediately. YIELD: 3 SERVINGS.

Eggs Benedict with Blender Hollandaise Sauce

BLENDER HOLLANDAISE:
4 egg yolks
1 tablespoon lemon juice
1 dash each paprika,
 cayenne pepper, and salt
¼ cup butter, melted
¼ cup extra-virgin olive oil

EGGS:
6 eggs
Butter for greasing muffin tin
1 tablespoon water

Whisk egg yolks, lemon juice, seasonings, and butter until blended. Cook over very low heat, stirring constantly, until mixture starts to bubble. Remove from heat immediately and cool for 4 minutes. Pour into blender, cover, and blend on high speed. Remove cover and blend on low while adding oil slowly in thin stream until sauce is thick and smooth. Scrape sides often. If making sauce ahead, refrigerate and heat over hot—not boiling—water while eggs are being prepared. Grease muffin cups with butter and crack 1 egg into each cup. Set muffin tin on jelly roll pan and pour water around tin's base. Bake at 350 degrees until set to your liking. Fork out onto individual plates and top with warm Hollandaise Sauce. YIELD: 6 SERVINGS.

Eggs in the Hole

2 tablespoons butter
2 thick slices bread
2 eggs

1 dash each salt, pepper, celery salt,
 and paprika

In large skillet, melt butter evenly. Using paring knife or biscuit cutter, cut 3-inch hole in middle of each slice of bread. Place slices side by side in pan. Over low heat, brown bread on first side and flip, moving it around to absorb remaining butter. Immediately crack 1 egg into each hole and add seasonings. Cook on medium heat until done. YIELD: 2 SERVINGS.

German Oven Pancake

3 eggs, lightly beaten
½ cup flour
½ cup milk
1 tablespoon butter, melted

½ teaspoon salt
2 tablespoons butter, melted
Powdered sugar

Combine eggs in mixing bowl. Gradually add flour to eggs, whisking until smooth. Stir in milk, 1 tablespoon melted butter, and salt. Grease 9-inch iron skillet or pie pan. Pour batter into cold skillet or pan. Bake at 450 degrees for 20 minutes. Brush with melted butter and sprinkle with powdered sugar.

Energy Bars

½ cup butter, room temperature

1¼ cups brown sugar

6 cups old-fashioned rolled oats

1 cup raisins

1 cup dried cranberries (such as Craisins)

1½ cups chopped dried fruit: apricots, pineapple, cherries, etc.

2 teaspoons cinnamon

½ teaspoon nutmeg

1 teaspoon salt

⅔ cup vanilla or strawberry protein powder

⅔ cup flaxseed meal

1 cup salted peanuts

1 cup egg whites, from carton

1 cup natural peanut or almond butter

1 (14 ounce) can sweetened condensed milk

In large bowl, cut butter into brown sugar until coarse. Stir in oats, raisins, dried fruit, cinnamon, nutmeg, salt, protein powder, flaxseed meal, and peanuts. In separate bowl, combine egg whites, peanut butter, and condensed milk, whisking until smooth. Add to oat mixture and stir until well blended. Line two jelly roll pans with parchment and press mixture into them. Bake at 350 degrees for 20 minutes. Allow to cool in pans. Then grasp parchment at either end and lift slabs out onto hard surface. Cut into bars. These freeze well in snack-size ziplock bags. YIELD: 3 DOZEN.

Gingerbread Waffles

1 cup light molasses
½ cup butter
1½ teaspoons baking soda
1½ cups milk
1 egg
2 cups flour

1½ teaspoons ginger
½ teaspoon cinnamon
½ teaspoon salt
Hot Chocolate Sauce
   (recipe follows)
Whipped topping

Preheat waffle iron and spray with nonstick cooking spray. In small saucepan, heat molasses and butter until almost boiling. Remove from heat and let cool slightly. Stir in baking soda, milk, and egg; set aside. In large bowl, mix flour, ginger, cinnamon, and salt. Make a well in the center and pour in molasses mixture. Mix until smooth. Pour batter onto hot waffle iron. Cook until golden brown. Serve with Hot Chocolate Sauce and whipped topping if desired.

HOT CHOCOLATE SAUCE:

2 cups boiling water
1 cup sugar
2 tablespoons cornstarch
½ cup cocoa

1 teaspoon salt
2 teaspoons vanilla
2 tablespoons butter

In medium saucepan, combine boiling water, sugar, cornstarch, cocoa, and salt. Cook over medium heat, stirring constantly, until mixture comes to a boil. Remove from heat and add vanilla and butter; stir until smooth.

Ginger Pear Jam

¼ pound fresh gingerroot
1½ cups cold water
3 pounds fully ripe pears
2 tablespoons lemon juice

1 (1¾ ounce) box powdered
  fruit pectin
5 cups sugar

Peel and chop gingerroot. Place in saucepan and add water; bring to a boil and continue boiling gently for 15 minutes. Drain; cover with cold water and let stand for 10 minutes. Drain again and measure ½ cup of ginger liquid. Peel, core, and finely chop pears. In saucepan stir together all ingredients except sugar. Over high heat, stirring constantly, bring mixture to a boil. Immediately add sugar; stirring constantly, bring to a full rolling boil and boil for 1 minute. Remove from heat and skim off foam. Pour into hot 8-ounce glass jars, filling to within ¼ inch of tops; cover and process in a boiling water bath for 5 minutes. YIELD: ABOUT 8 (8 OUNCE) JARS.

As a Gift: This jam makes a beautiful gift in a clear glass jar so the light can shine through. Find lids that match the season and tie with a colorful bow. Your friends will love it and ask for more next year.

Glazed Breakfast Fruit

4 pears, quartered
4 peaches, quartered
6 apricots, quartered

1 cup brown sugar or to taste
4 tablespoons butter

Place quartered fruits in shallow baking dish. Sprinkle with brown sugar; dot with butter. Bake at 450 degrees for 15 to 20 minutes until bubbly. (May use canned fruit.)

Granola

4 cups quick-cooking oats
1½ cups wheat germ
¼ cup powdered milk
2 teaspoons cinnamon
1 tablespoon brown sugar
⅓ cup canola oil

½ cup honey
1 tablespoon vanilla
½ cup sesame seeds (optional)
½ cup raw nuts, seeds, or raisins
  (optional)

Mix dry ingredients in large bowl and set aside. In saucepan over low heat, combine oil, honey, and vanilla. Add to dry ingredients. Stir until all particles are coated. Spread in greased jelly roll pan. Bake at 250 degrees for 1 hour or at 300 degrees for 30 minutes, stirring with spatula occasionally. Cool and store in airtight container.

Overnight French Toast

½ cup chopped pecans
1 cup plus 1 tablespoon brown
  sugar
½ cup butter
2 tablespoons maple pancake syrup
  (not pure maple syrup)
12 slices white bread

6 eggs, beaten
1½ cups milk
1 teaspoon vanilla
½ teaspoon cinnamon
½ teaspoon salt

Spray 9x13-inch pan with nonstick cooking spray; spread pecans evenly on bottom of pan. In saucepan, combine brown sugar, butter, and syrup and cook until thick; pour mixture over pecans. Place 6 slices of bread on top of mixture; layer remaining 6 slices over first layer. Combine eggs, milk, vanilla, cinnamon, and salt. Pour over bread slices. Chill for at least 8 hours. Bake at 350 degrees for 40 to 45 minutes.

Grandma's Sausage Gravy and Country Biscuits

GRAVY:

1 pound seasoned pork sausage

2 tablespoons flour

2 cups milk

Salt and pepper to taste

Brown sausage and drain, reserving 2 tablespoons grease; set aside reserved grease for biscuit recipe below. Stir flour into browned sausage and gradually add milk. Continue stirring over medium heat until gravy thickens. Add salt and pepper. Serve over split Country Biscuits (recipe follows).

COUNTRY BISCUITS:

2 cups flour

½ teaspoon salt

3 teaspoons baking powder

⅓ cup shortening

1 cup milk

2 tablespoons reserved pork grease (from gravy recipe above)

Sift dry ingredients into mixing bowl. Using pastry blender or fork, cut in ⅓ cup shortening until mixture resembles coarse crumbs. Add milk and mix until dough forms soft ball. Turn out on lightly floured surface; knead gently for 1 minute. Roll to ½-inch thickness and cut with 2-inch round cutter. Pour 2 tablespoons reserved grease into baking pan. Place biscuits in pan, turning so each side gets greased. Bake at 450 degrees until golden brown, about 15 minutes. YIELD: 12 TO 15 BISCUITS.

Holiday Breakfast Grits

1 quart eggnog
5 tablespoons butter
1 cup uncooked grits

1 teaspoon salt
2 cups fresh blueberries

In large saucepan, warm eggnog and butter over low heat. Add grits and salt slowly while stirring. Keep stirring for about 25 minutes or until bubbly. Add blueberries and cook for 5 more minutes.

Maple Syrup

1 cup hot water
1 cup sugar

1 cup brown sugar
1 teaspoon maple flavoring

Mix in blender until sugar is dissolved.

Oven-Baked Omelet

6 eggs, lightly beaten
½ cup cottage cheese
½ cup sour cream
½ cup mild salsa

1 cup shredded Monterey Jack cheese
1 cup shredded cheddar cheese

Mix first 3 ingredients in large bowl and set aside. Spray casserole dish with nonstick cooking spray. Spread salsa in bottom of dish and add cheeses. Pour egg mixture over cheese. Bake at 350 degrees for 45 minutes.

Potato Pancakes (Latkes)

6 medium potatoes
1 small onion, chopped
2 eggs, beaten
3 tablespoons flour

½ teaspoon baking powder
1 teaspoon salt
½ teaspoon pepper
1 dash paprika

Peel and grate potatoes. Drain off any liquid and add chopped onion, eggs, and remaining ingredients. Mix well and drop 1 tablespoon at a time onto hot, greased griddle. Brown both sides and drain on paper towels. Serve with sour cream, chives, shredded cheese, crumbled bacon, or sliced ham. YIELD: 1 DOZEN LATKES.

Sausage and Cheese Grits Casserole

4 cups water
1 teaspoon salt
1 cup quick-cooking grits
4 eggs, beaten
1 pound pork sausage, browned

1½ cups shredded cheddar cheese, divided
1 cup milk
½ cup margarine

Grease 3-quart baking dish and set aside. Bring water and salt to a boil in large saucepan. Slowly stir in grits; cook for 4 to 5 minutes, stirring occasionally. Remove from heat. Lightly beat eggs in large bowl and stir grits mixture into eggs; return all to saucepan. Add sausage, 1 cup cheese, milk, and margarine; blend well. Pour into baking dish; sprinkle with remaining ½ cup cheese. Bake at 350 degrees for about 1 hour. Let stand for 10 minutes before serving.

Matchless Coconut Almond Granola

8 cups old-fashioned rolled oats
1 cup slivered or sliced almonds
1 cup unsweetened coconut
    shavings
½ cup raw sesame seeds
½ cup raw pumpkin seeds
½ cup raw sunflower seeds

¾ cup pure maple syrup
½ cup coconut oil
¼ cup honey
1 tablespoon molasses
1 tablespoon vanilla
2 teaspoons cinnamon
1 teaspoon sea salt

Combine oats, almonds, coconut shavings, and seeds in large bowl. In separate bowl, stir together remaining ingredients and pour over dry ingredients. Mix well. Line two large jelly roll pans with parchment paper. Pour half of granola onto each pan and spread evenly. Bake at 340 degrees for 12 minutes, toss granola gently, and continue baking at 325 degrees for 30 minutes longer, stirring every 10 minutes. Cool on pans and store in airtight containers. YIELD: 10 CUPS.

Swedish Oven Pancakes

½ cup butter
4 eggs
1 teaspoon salt

4 cups milk
2 cups flour

Heat oven to 400 degrees and place butter in 9x13-inch pan to melt in oven. In large bowl, combine all other ingredients and pour into hot buttered pan. Bake for 35 to 40 minutes or until set. Serve with syrup.

Parfait Fruit Cups

1 cup granola
1 cup plain Greek yogurt
1 cup diced fruit or berries

Layer ingredients twice in order given in clear parfait glasses. YIELD: 2 PARFAITS.

Pear Breakfast Cake

¼ cup shortening
½ cup sugar
1 egg
½ teaspoon vanilla
1 cup flour
1 teaspoon baking powder

½ teaspoon baking soda
½ teaspoon salt
¼ teaspoon nutmeg
½ cup sour cream
¾ cup finely chopped ripe pear

TOPPING:
½ cup chopped walnuts
¼ cup brown sugar

½ teaspoon cinnamon
2 tablespoons butter, melted

Cream together shortening, sugar, egg, and vanilla. In separate bowl, blend flour, baking powder, baking soda, salt, and nutmeg. Add to creamed mixture along with sour cream and pears. Pour into 8x8-inch baking dish. Mix together topping ingredients until crumbly. Sprinkle over cake and bake at 350 degrees for 30 minutes. YIELD: 6 SERVINGS.

South-of-the-Border Breakfast Casserole

1 cup pork sausage
½ cup diced onion
¾ cup butter
6 slices bread, cubed
10 eggs
2½ cups whole milk

1 small can green chilies
1 teaspoon salt
1 teaspoon pepper
1½ cups shredded Mexican-style
   cheese

In large skillet, brown sausage and onion. Drain on paper towels. Add butter to pan and sauté bread cubes. Pour into casserole dish. In large bowl, beat together eggs, milk, green chilies, salt, and pepper until frothy. Pour half of mixture over bread; add half of cheese. Repeat layers. Bake uncovered at 325 degrees for 45 minutes. YIELD: 10 SERVINGS.

Waffles

3 cups sifted flour

4 teaspoons double-acting
   baking powder

1 teaspoon salt

2 teaspoons sugar

4 eggs, separated

⅔ cup butter, margarine,
   or vegetable oil

1 teaspoon vanilla

2 cups milk

Sift together dry ingredients and set aside. In mixing bowl, beat egg whites until stiff. Beat egg yolks in separate bowl for 1 minute. Melt butter or margarine; set aside to cool. Add vanilla and milk to egg yolks and combine with dry ingredients; mix until blended. Add cooled butter or oil. Fold in egg whites. Pour batter into preheated waffle iron. YIELD: 4 LARGE OR 8 SMALL WAFFLES.

Whole-Wheat Muffins

2 cups whole-wheat flour

½ teaspoon baking soda

½ teaspoon salt

3 tablespoons sugar

1 cup milk

1 tablespoon lemon juice or vinegar

3 tablespoons butter, melted

Sift flour into bowl; add baking soda, salt, and sugar. Sift again and set aside. In separate bowl, mix together milk and lemon juice or vinegar; let stand for 5 minutes before adding milk mixture and then butter to flour mixture. Spoon into greased muffin tins. Bake at 400 degrees for 25 minutes.

Brunch

Apple Cake

⅔ cup vegetable oil
2 eggs
3 cups peeled and chopped
    tart apples
1½ cups sugar

1¾ cups flour
1 teaspoon baking soda
½ teaspoon salt
2 teaspoons cinnamon
2 teaspoons vanilla

In mixing bowl, beat oil and eggs until foamy. Stir in apples and sugar. In separate bowl, mix flour, soda, salt, and cinnamon. Stir into apple mixture. Stir in vanilla. Bake in a 9x13-inch pan at 325 degrees for 45 minutes.

Apple Ring

½ cup sugar
1 teaspoon cinnamon
2 tubes refrigerated buttermilk
    biscuits (20 total)

½ cup butter, melted
1 apple, peeled, cored, and sliced
    into 20 slices

Mix together sugar and cinnamon. Dip each biscuit in butter and then in sugar mixture. Place 15 biscuits around outer edge of greased 9-inch round cake pan. Place remaining 5 in the center. Slide a slice of apple between each biscuit; pour remaining sugar and butter (if any remains) on top. Bake at 350 degrees for 25 to 30 minutes. Invert onto serving platter immediately, being careful, as butter may drip out.

Apple Cream Scones

2 cups chopped tart apples
6 tablespoons butter, divided
1 tablespoon instant coffee granules
1 teaspoon hot water
½ cup whipped cream

2¼ cups flour
⅓ cup sugar
1 tablespoon baking powder
¼ teaspoon salt
2 tablespoons coarse sugar

Cook apples in 2 tablespoons butter until tender and liquid is almost evaporated, stirring often; cool slightly. Dissolve coffee in hot water and stir in whipped cream; set aside. Mix flour, sugar, baking powder, and salt; cut in remaining 4 tablespoons butter until mixture resembles coarse crumbs. Add apples and coffee mixture; stir just until dough clings together. On lightly floured surface, knead 6 times. On ungreased baking sheet, pat dough into 8-inch circle. Top with coarse sugar. Cut into 8 or 10 wedges; separate slightly. Bake at 400 degrees for 20 to 25 minutes. Cool slightly; serve warm.

Apple Dumplings

2 cups flour
1 heaping teaspoon baking powder
½ teaspoon salt
⅓ cup shortening
Milk, enough to moisten to
  pie dough consistency

3 apples, peeled, cored, and halved
4 tablespoons sugar
1 teaspoon cinnamon
½ cup brown sugar
2 tablespoons butter
¾ cup boiling water

Combine first 4 ingredients in large bowl; add enough milk to moisten. Roll to ¼ inch thick. Cut into 6 pieces. Put half an apple on each piece. Sprinkle with sugar and cinnamon. Wrap dough around apple and place in deep baking pan with brown sugar sprinkled on the bottom. Before putting in oven, melt butter in boiling water and pour over dumplings. Bake at 350 degrees for 30 to 35 minutes.

Apple Walnut Squares

2 cups flour
1 teaspoon salt
1 teaspoon baking soda
½ teaspoon cinnamon
3 eggs

1¾ cups sugar
1 cup vegetable oil
1 teaspoon vanilla
2 cups pared, diced apples
¾ cup chopped walnuts

Sift together first 4 ingredients; set aside. In mixing bowl, blend eggs, sugar, oil, and vanilla. Stir in sifted ingredients; mix well. Fold in apples and nuts and pour into lightly greased 9x13-inch pan. Bake at 325 degrees for 1 hour.

Breakfast Sausage Bake

2½ cups croutons
2 cups shredded cheddar cheese
1 pound bulk pork sausage
4 eggs, beaten

¾ teaspoon dry mustard
2½ cups milk
1 (10.5 ounce) can condensed
  cream of mushroom soup

Place croutons in greased 9x13-inch dish. Top with cheese. Brown sausage in skillet; drain on paper towel. Spread sausage over cheese. In mixing bowl, beat eggs. Mix in mustard, milk, and mushroom soup. Pour over sausage. Bake at 300 degrees for 90 minutes. May be refrigerated overnight before baking.

Butterscotch Coffee Cake

1 cup chopped pecans
1 package frozen yeast dinner rolls
  (about 20 rolls)
1 small package butterscotch
  pudding (not instant)

½ cup butter or margarine
½ cup brown sugar
½ cup sugar

Spray Bundt pan with nonstick cooking spray. Sprinkle nuts in bottom of pan. Separate frozen rolls and distribute evenly in pan. Sprinkle dry pudding over rolls. Melt butter and mix with sugars. Pour over top. Cover with towel and let rise overnight or 8 hours. Cover with foil; bake at 350 degrees for 30 minutes. Remove foil and bake for another 10 minutes. Allow to cool in pan a few minutes; invert onto large serving platter, keeping pan in place for a few minutes before removing.

Norwegian Coffee Cake

4 cups flour
6 teaspoons baking powder
1 cup sugar
½ teaspoon salt
1 cup butter or margarine

2 eggs
1 cup milk
Frosting (optional)
1 cup chopped walnuts

Sift together dry ingredients. Blend in butter as for piecrust. Beat eggs and milk in separate bowl. Add to dry ingredients; don't overmix. Grease two 9-inch round cake pans and put half of mixture into each pan by putting spoonfuls around the edge. Bake at 400 degrees for 20 minutes. Frost if desired; sprinkle with nuts.

Date Rolls

1 cup butter
1½ cups sugar
1 pound dates, cut up
2 eggs, lightly beaten
1 teaspoon vanilla

3 tablespoons milk
1½ cups chopped pecans
4 cups toasted rice cereal
¼ cup coconut

Melt butter in skillet. Dissolve sugar in butter; add dates. Stir until thick. Slowly add eggs, vanilla, and milk to pan. Stir in pecans and cereal. Form into ovals; roll in coconut. Store in cool place.

Christmas Wreath Coffee Cake

BATTER:
1½ cups flour, sifted
2½ teaspoons baking powder
½ teaspoon salt
1 egg, lightly beaten
¾ cup sugar
⅓ cup shortening, melted
½ cup milk
1 teaspoon vanilla

STREUSEL:
½ cup firmly packed brown sugar
2 tablespoons flour
1 teaspoon cinnamon
2 teaspoons shortening

GLAZE:
1 tablespoon milk
1 cup powdered sugar, sifted
½ teaspoon vanilla

Sift together flour, baking powder, and salt; set aside. Combine remaining batter ingredients in separate bowl. Stir into flour mixture just until blended. Set aside. Make streusel by combining brown sugar, flour, and cinnamon. Cut in shortening until crumbly. Place half of streusel in greased 1-quart ring mold; top with half of batter. Repeat layers. Bake at 375 degrees for 30 minutes. Cool for 10 minutes in mold. Invert on wire rack and cool completely. Combine all glaze ingredients; stir to blend well. Drizzle cake with glaze.

Fruit Dip

1 (8 ounce) package cream cheese, softened
½ cup powdered sugar (add a little more if needed)
¼ cup lemon juice
2 tablespoons milk

Mix all ingredients together until smooth. Serve with fresh fruit.

Christmas Braid

½ cup butter
1½ cups buttermilk
2 packages yeast
½ cup sugar
½ teaspoon salt
4 cups flour, divided

½ cup strawberry jam, divided
1 egg, beaten
½ cup powdered sugar
1 tablespoon water
Candied cherries

In medium saucepan, heat butter and buttermilk to melt butter. Pour into large bowl and cool to 105 to 115 degrees. Sprinkle yeast over warm milk; stir to dissolve. Add sugar, salt, and half of flour. Beat at medium speed until smooth. With wooden spoon or pastry hooks of mixer, add remaining flour. Knead by hand or machine for 5 minutes. Place in lightly greased bowl. Cover and let rise for 45 to 60 minutes. Knead again until smooth. Separate into 3 balls. Roll each into rectangle about 15 inches long. Spread one-third of jam in center of each rectangle. Transfer rectangles to baking sheets or 9x13-inch pans, placing pans side by side. Make diagonal slits down both sides of each rectangle, each about 4 inches long. Fold these "flaps" alternately over jam to create braided appearance. Let rise for 1 more hour or until desired size. Brush with beaten egg and bake at 375 degrees for 20 to 25 minutes; cool. Combine powdered sugar and water and drizzle over each braid. Decorate with candied cherries to look like holly and berries.

Hot Peach Marlow

6 peach halves (canned or fresh)
1 cup canned crushed pineapple
6 large marshmallows

Preheat broiler. Place peach halves in baking dish cut side up. Fill peach halves with pineapple and top with marshmallows. Broil until marshmallows are golden brown. Serve hot.

Orange Date Bars

FILLING:
15 candy orange slices, cut up
½ cup sugar
1 cup dates, cut up
2½ tablespoons flour
1 cup hot water

BATTER:
1 cup brown sugar
½ cup shortening
2 eggs
1 teaspoon vanilla
1¾ cups flour
1 teaspoon baking soda

Combine all filling ingredients and cook until thick. Cool slightly. To make batter, combine sugar and shortening; add eggs and beat. Add remaining ingredients. Put half of mixture in greased 9x13-inch pan. Spread with orange/date mixture. Cover with remaining batter. Bake at 350 degrees for 30 to 35 minutes.

Rhubarb Crunch

CRUMB MIXTURE:
1 cup sifted flour
½ cup butter, melted
¾ cup old-fashioned rolled oats
1 teaspoon cinnamon
1 cup brown sugar

FRUIT MIXTURE:
4 cups diced rhubarb
1 cup water
1 cup sugar
1 teaspoon vanilla
2 tablespoons cornstarch

Mix crumb mixture ingredients until crumbly. Press half of crumbs into greased 9x9-inch pan. Cover with rhubarb. In small saucepan, combine water, sugar, vanilla, and cornstarch. Cook over medium heat, stirring until thick and clear. Pour sauce over rhubarb; top with remaining crumbs. Bake at 350 degrees for 1 hour.

Raspberry Bars

CRUST:
1 package white or yellow cake mix
½ cup butter, softened

LAYER:
½ cup raspberry preserves

FILLING:
1 (8 ounce) package cream
  cheese, softened
¼ cup sugar
2 tablespoons all-purpose flour
1 teaspoon vanilla
1 egg
¼ cup raspberry preserves

Combine cake mix and butter; mix with fork until crumbly. Reserve 1 cup for topping. Press remaining mixture in bottom of greased 9x13-inch pan. Carefully spread ½ cup preserves over crust. In mixing bowl, combine cream cheese, sugar, flour, vanilla, egg, and ¼ cup preserves. Mix until well blended. Spread evenly over preserves layer. Sprinkle with reserved topping. Bake at 350 degrees for 30 to 40 minutes. Cool for at least 1 hour; cut into bars.

Spinach Mushroom Quiche

1 (10 ounce) bag fresh spinach
1 frozen piecrust, thawed
1½ ounces bacon bits
1 can mushrooms, drained

8 eggs
⅔ cup milk
2 cups shredded cheddar cheese

Place spinach in crust; add bacon bits and mushrooms. Combine eggs and milk in mixing bowl; pour mixture into piecrust. Top with cheese. Bake at 350 degrees for 50 minutes.

Tuna Cheese Crescent Squares

1 tube refrigerated crescent rolls, unseparated
1 (8 ounce) package cream cheese, softened
¼ cup butter or margarine
1 cup chopped onion
½ teaspoon dry mustard
½ teaspoon salt
¼ teaspoon pepper
1 (6½ ounce) can tuna, drained
8 ounces shredded cheddar cheese

Press crescent rolls on bottom and up sides of 6x10-inch baking dish. In small bowl, mix cream cheese and butter. Add next 5 ingredients, stirring to combine. Spread onto dough layer. Top with cheese. Bake at 375 degrees for 20 minutes. Cool for 5 minutes before cutting into squares.

Tuna Quiche

1 (6½ ounce) can tuna, drained and flaked
1 cup shredded white cheddar cheese
3 ounces cream cheese, cut up
3 tablespoons sliced green onions
1 (2 ounce) jar chopped pimentos, drained
2 cups milk
1 cup all-purpose baking mix
4 eggs
¾ teaspoon salt
Dash nutmeg

In mixing bowl, combine tuna, cheeses, onions, and pimentos. Transfer to greased 10-inch pie pan. Beat remaining ingredients in blender on high for 15 seconds. Pour into pie pan. Bake at 400 degrees for 35 to 40 minutes, until knife comes out clean.

CHRISTMAS DINNER
Including
MAIN DISHES
and SIDES

I will honor Christmas in my heart
and try to keep it all the year.
CHARLES DICKENS

Jesus, life with You is sweeter each day!
Open our arms and hearts to include the lonely
and forgotten ones all around us, and fill every
soul to the brim with the gifts of Your warm,
welcoming grace. Amen.

*I will be fully satisfied as with the
richest of foods; with singing lips
my mouth will praise you.*

PSALM 63:5 NIV

Main Dishes

Baked Pork Chops and Apples

4 to 6 apples, peeled and sliced
½ cup brown sugar
2 tablespoons flour
½ teaspoon cinnamon
¼ teaspoon nutmeg
6 pork chops, browned

In mixing bowl, combine apples, brown sugar, flour, and spices. Transfer to oblong baking dish. Top with browned pork chops. Cover and bake at 375 degrees for 1½ hours. Serve with apples and sauce on top of pork chops.

Chicken Diane

4 large boneless chicken
  breast halves
½ teaspoon salt
½ teaspoon pepper
2 tablespoons olive oil, divided
2 tablespoons butter or
  margarine, divided
3 tablespoons chopped fresh chives
3 tablespoons chopped fresh parsley
Juice of ½ lemon
2 teaspoons Dijon mustard
¼ cup chicken broth

Place each chicken breast between two sheets of waxed paper and pound to flatten slightly. Sprinkle chicken with salt and pepper. Set aside. In large skillet, heat 1 tablespoon each of oil and butter. Cook chicken breasts in skillet for 4 minutes on each side. Transfer to warm serving platter. Add chives, parsley, lemon juice, and mustard to skillet. Cook for 15 seconds, whisking constantly. Whisk in chicken broth and stir until sauce is smooth. Whisk in remaining 1 tablespoon each of oil and butter. Pour sauce over chicken and serve immediately. YIELD: 4 SERVINGS.

Chicken Orange

1 chicken, cut into pieces
Herbs as desired
½ cup butter, melted

1 (12 ounce) can frozen orange
  juice concentrate

Remove skin from chicken and arrange pieces in baking dish. Sprinkle with herbs. Combine melted butter and undiluted orange juice; pour over chicken. Bake uncovered at 350 degrees for 1 hour.

Cornish Hens
with Basil-Walnut Sauce

1 bunch fresh basil
½ cup grated parmesan cheese
1 clove garlic
Salt and pepper to taste
¼ cup walnuts
2 Cornish game hens, split and
  quartered

Butter
½ cup chicken stock
½ cup heavy cream
Additional basil and walnuts
for garnish

In food processor basket, combine first 5 ingredients. Puree to smooth paste; set aside. In large skillet, cook hens in butter until tender. Transfer to warm platter. Drain grease from skillet and pour in chicken stock. Cook until stock is reduced by half. Add cream and again reduce to half. Stir in 2 tablespoons of basil-walnut paste. Add additional salt and pepper if needed. Pour sauce over hens and garnish with basil and walnuts. YIELD: 4 SERVINGS.

Creamy Chicken
and Rice with Thyme

¾ cup chicken broth or water
½ teaspoon salt
1½ cups quick-cooking rice
1½ to 2 pounds split chicken breast
1 (6 ounce) can sliced mushrooms,
  with liquid

1 (10.5 ounce) can condensed
  cream of mushroom soup
½ teaspoon thyme
1 tablespoon fine bread crumbs
1 tablespoon butter, melted

In greased roasting pan, combine first 3 ingredients. Place chicken over rice mixture. Combine mushrooms and soup. Spread over chicken. Sprinkle with thyme, bread crumbs, and butter. Cover tightly with foil and bake at 400 degrees for 1 hour or until chicken is done. YIELD: 4 SERVINGS.

Glazed Ham

1 (7 to 10 pound) fully cooked ham   1 teaspoon cinnamon
1 (2 liter) bottle Dr Pepper   Whole cloves
1 tablespoon ground cloves

Place ham in roasting pan and cover with mixture of Dr Pepper, ground cloves, and cinnamon. Bake at 325 degrees for 1½ hours. Remove from oven and score top of ham. Stud ham with whole cloves.

MIX TOGETHER:
1 teaspoon cinnamon
1 teaspoon dry mustard
Dr Pepper

Add enough Dr Pepper to form paste. Brush mixture over scored ham.

MIX TOGETHER:
1 cup brown sugar
¼ cup Dr Pepper (or enough to form paste)

Brush final mixture over ham. Bake for another 1½ hours or until meat thermometer reads 140 degrees. YIELD: 12 TO 14 SERVINGS.

Herbed Cornish Hens

3 Rock Cornish hens (about 1
   pound each), thawed
Salt and pepper
¼ cup butter or margarine, melted

½ teaspoon dried marjoram
½ teaspoon dried thyme
¼ teaspoon paprika
Watercress for garnish

Rub cavities of hens with salt and pepper. Combine margarine, marjoram, thyme, and paprika; brush portion of mixture on hens that have been placed in shallow baking pan, breast side up. Roast uncovered at 350 degrees, brushing with remaining margarine mixture 5 or 6 times until done (about 1 hour). Cut each hen into halves with scissors, cutting along backbone from tail to neck and down center of breast. Garnish with watercress.

Festive Holiday Ham

1 (7 pound) smoked ham
2 cups water
Olive oil
Whole cloves
1 cup brown sugar
2 tablespoons flour
⅛ teaspoon garlic powder

⅛ teaspoon onion powder
⅛ teaspoon pepper
1 (16 ounce) can sliced pineapple rings
1 jar maraschino cherries, cut into halves

Place ham in roasting pan with water. Cover and bake at 325 degrees for 3½ to 4½ hours. If ham has exposed bone, cover with foil. Spray ham occasionally with olive oil during first part of cooking. Continue roasting until thermometer inserted in center reads 160 degrees. Be sure thermometer is not touching bone. When ham is done, remove from oven. Lift off rind. Using sharp knife, score fat surface crosswise and dot with cloves. Set aside. Combine brown sugar and flour. Rub mixture over scored ham. Sprinkle lightly with garlic powder, onion powder, and pepper. Place pineapple slices on ham with cloves in center. Cover cloves with maraschino cherry half. Continue until ham is covered decoratively with pineapple slices and cherries. Bake uncovered at 400 degrees for 20 minutes.

Country Holiday Ham

1 (7 pound) sugar-cured ham
Whole cloves

2 cups maple pancake syrup (not pure maple syrup)
½ cup cola

Remove skin from ham. Score fat surface of ham with knife in diamond shape or any design and stud with cloves. Pour syrup and then cola over ham. Cover with foil and bake at 350 degrees for 3 to 4 hours, checking after 3 hours to make sure ham isn't getting dry.

Ham with Apple Relish

1 teaspoon ground cloves
1 (3 to 4 pound) fully cooked bone-less ham
4 medium tart apples, peeled and chopped
2 cups sugar
1 cup chopped dried apricots
½ cup dried cranberries
½ cup golden raisins
¼ cup white vinegar
2 tablespoons grated orange peel
½ teaspoon ginger

Rub cloves over ham. Wrap ham tightly in foil and bake at 325 degrees for 1 to 1½ hours or until meat thermometer reads 140 degrees. Meanwhile, combine remaining ingredients in saucepan. Stirring constantly, bring mixture to a boil. Reduce heat and simmer for 25 to 30 minutes or until thickened. Serve relish over ham slices. YIELD: 8 TO 10 SERVINGS.

Holiday Ham Casserole

3 tablespoons butter
2 cups cubed cooked ham
1 (8.5 ounce) can pineapple chunks, drained
1 (10.5 ounce) can condensed french onion soup
3 tablespoons brown sugar, divided
Salt and pepper to taste
1 (10.5 ounce) can sweet potatoes, drained
½ cup chopped walnuts

In large saucepan, heat butter and ham until lightly browned. Add pineapple chunks, onion soup, and 1 tablespoon brown sugar. Season with salt and pepper to taste. Bring to a boil, remove from heat and spoon into buttered casserole dish. Place sweet potato slices in even layer over ham and pineapple mixture. Combine walnuts and remaining 2 tablespoons brown sugar. Spread over sweet potatoes. Bake at 400 degrees for 30 minutes.

Home-Style Turkey

1 (12 to 14 pound) whole turkey
6 tablespoons butter, divided
3 tablespoons chicken bouillon
4 cups warm water

2 tablespoons dried minced onion
2 tablespoons parsley flakes
2 tablespoons seasoned salt

Rinse turkey and remove giblet packet from inside. Put turkey on rack in roasting pan. Cut 6 pockets into skin over each breast and insert 1 tablespoon butter in each pocket. In large bowl, dissolve bouillon in water; add onion and parsley. Pour over turkey. Sprinkle seasoned salt over entire turkey. Cover with foil and bake at 350 degrees for 3 hours; remove foil. Bake for another 30 to 60 minutes or until meat thermometer reads 180 degrees. Remove and let rest for 15 minutes before carving.

Venison Roast

1 (3 to 5 pound) venison roast
¼ teaspoon pepper
¼ teaspoon salt
¼ cup vegetable oil
2 (10.5 ounce) cans condensed
cream of mushroom soup

1 envelope dry onion soup mix
1½ cups water
1 (6.5 ounce) can mushrooms,
drained
2 cloves garlic, minced

Sprinkle meat with pepper and salt. In skillet, brown all sides of roast in oil. Combine soups and water; add mushrooms and garlic; pour over roast. Transfer to slow cooker and cook on low for about 6 hours or until meat easily pulls apart. Or bake in dutch oven at 375 degrees for 3 to 4 hours.

Italian Turkey

1½ pounds ground salt pork
1 garlic clove, minced
3 teaspoons sage

2½ to 3⅓ teaspoons chili powder
Salt and pepper to taste
1 (10 to 12 pound) turkey

Combine first 5 ingredients and spread over turkey. Bake at 350 degrees for 4½ hours or until done. Remove pork mixture from turkey and place in large bowl; crumble mixture with fork. Debone turkey and chop meat into small pieces. Blend turkey with pork mixture. Serve as loose meat or with rolls for sandwiches. YIELD: 25 TO 30 SERVINGS.

Home-Style Roast Beef

1 (10 to 12 pound) bottom round beef roast
1 (14.5 ounce) can chicken broth
1 (10.25 ounce) can beef gravy
1 (10.5 ounce) can condensed cream of celery soup
¼ cup water
¼ cup Worcestershire sauce
¼ cup soy sauce

3 tablespoons parsley flakes
3 tablespoons dill weed
2 tablespoons thyme
4½ teaspoons garlic powder
1 teaspoon celery salt
1 teaspoon pepper
1 large onion, sliced into rings

Place roast in large roasting pan, fat side up. Prick meat with meat fork. In mixing bowl, combine broth, gravy, soup, water, Worcestershire, and soy sauce. Pour mixture evenly over roast; then sprinkle with seasonings. Place onion rings over roast. Bake uncovered at 325 degrees for 2½ to 3½ hours or until meat reaches desired doneness. Meat thermometer should read 140 degrees for a rare roast, 160 degrees for a medium roast, and 170 degrees for a well-done roast. Let stand for 15 to 20 minutes before slicing. YIELD: 25 TO 30 SERVINGS.

Honey Roast Ham

1 (4½ pound) cured ham, leg or
   shoulder roast
1 onion
Cloves
2 bay leaves
Few black peppercorns
Few parsley stems
Twist of orange peel
Small piece of fresh ginger
½ cinnamon stick

GLAZE:
6 tablespoons clear honey
2 tablespoons whole grain mustard

Calculate cooking time for ham, figuring 20 minutes per pound, adding an extra 20 minutes. To draw off salt used in curing process, place ham in large pot and cover with cold water. Bring to a boil and remove from heat. Pour off water and replace with fresh cold water, adding onion, cloves, and remaining flavoring ingredients. Bring to a boil slowly; cover and simmer for calculated time, subtracting 15 minutes. Transfer ham to roasting pan and cool slightly. Heat oven to 350 degrees. With sharp knife, score fat of ham in diamond pattern and stud with cloves. Combine honey and mustard and spread over skin. Wrap ham in foil, leaving glazed area uncovered. Bake for 15 minutes. Serve hot or cold. YIELD: 8 TO 10 SERVINGS.

Huntington Chicken

4 cups chicken broth
8 tablespoons flour
½ pound processed cheese, grated
1 (4 to 5 pound) whole chicken,
   stewed and deboned
2 cups cooked macaroni
Salt and pepper to taste
7 slices bread, crumbled
¼ cup butter, melted

In large saucepan, heat broth. Blend 1 cup broth with flour to make paste. Return to pan of broth to create gravy. Stir in cheese until melted. Add chicken and macaroni. Transfer to ungreased 9x13-inch baking dish. Combine bread with butter and cover casserole. Bake at 350 degrees for 45 minutes or until bubbly. (Casserole may be frozen without topping prior to baking.)

Veal in Wine with Mushrooms

3 pounds veal, cut into 1-inch cubes
2 tablespoons butter
2 (4.5 ounce) cans mushroom caps
½ cup cooking oil
1 cup white wine

½ cup chopped onion
1 teaspoon oregano
1 cup sour cream
5½ cups cooked rice

Brown veal in butter. Add remaining ingredients except sour cream and rice; simmer for 30 to 40 minutes until tender. Remove from heat and add sour cream; serve with cooked rice.

Lasagna

1 pound Italian sausage
1 clove garlic, minced
1 tablespoon whole basil
1½ teaspoons salt
1 (1 pound) can tomatoes
2 (6 ounce) cans tomato paste
10 ounces lasagna noodles
2 eggs

3 cups fresh ricotta or cream-style cottage cheese
½ cup grated parmesan or romano cheese
2 tablespoons parsley flakes
1 teaspoon salt
½ teaspoon pepper
1 pound mozzarella cheese, thinly sliced

Brown sausage slowly and spoon off excess fat. Add next 5 ingredients plus 1 cup of water and simmer, covered, for 15 minutes; stir frequently. Cook noodles in boiling salted water until tender. Beat eggs and add remaining ingredients except mozzarella. Layer half of lasagna noodles in 9x13-inch baking dish; spread with half of ricotta filling, half of mozzarella cheese, and half of meat sauce. Repeat layers. Bake at 375 degrees for 30 minutes. YIELD: 8 TO 10 SERVINGS.

Savory Pork Roast

1 (4 pound) boneless top-loin pork roast
1 clove garlic, cut into halves

1 teaspoon salt
1 teaspoon sage
1 teaspoon marjoram

Rub pork roast with cut sides of garlic. Mix remaining ingredients and sprinkle on roast. Place fat side up in shallow roasting pan. Insert meat thermometer in thickest part of pork and roast uncovered at 325 degrees for 2 to 2½ hours or until meat thermometer reads 170 degrees. Garnish with frosted grapes (dipped in water and rolled in sugar) if desired.

Lemon-Herb Turkey Breast

1 (8 to 9 pound) bone-in turkey breast
3 tablespoons fresh lemon juice, divided
2 tablespoons olive oil, divided
2 cloves garlic, crushed
1¼ teaspoons salt
1 teaspoon grated lemon peel
1 teaspoon thyme
1 teaspoon freshly ground black pepper
½ teaspoon sage
Lemon-pepper seasoning to taste

Rinse turkey in cold water and pat dry. Loosen skin from turkey with fingers, but leave skin attached to meat. In small bowl, combine 1 tablespoon lemon juice, 1 tablespoon oil, garlic, salt, lemon peel, thyme, pepper, and sage. Spread evenly under turkey skin. Combine remaining 2 tablespoons lemon juice and 1 tablespoon oil; set aside. Place turkey on rack in shallow roasting pan sprayed with cooking spray. Bake uncovered at 350 degrees for 2½ to 3 hours or until meat thermometer reads 170 degrees, basting every 15 to 20 minutes with lemon juice and oil mixture. Let stand for 10 to 15 minutes before carving. Add lemon-pepper seasoning to taste as desired. YIELD: 16 SERVINGS.

Traditional Christmas Turkey

1 (10 to 12 pound) whole turkey
6 tablespoons butter, cut into slices
3 cubes chicken bouillon
4 cups warm water
2 tablespoons parsley flakes
2 tablespoons dried minced onion
2 tablespoons seasoned salt
2 tablespoons poultry seasoning

Rinse turkey. Remove neck and discard giblets. Place turkey in roasting pan. Separate skin over breast and place slices of butter between skin and breast meat. In small bowl, dissolve bouillon in water. Stir in parsley and minced onion and pour mixture over top of turkey. Sprinkle turkey with seasoned salt and poultry seasoning. Cover with foil and bake at 350 degrees for 3½ to 4 hours or until meat thermometer reads 180 degrees. Remove foil during last 45 minutes to brown turkey. YIELD: 12 SERVINGS.

Roast Beef with Yorkshire Pudding

1 (4 to 6 pound) boneless rib roast
Salt and pepper to taste

YORKSHIRE PUDDING BATTER
1 cup all-purpose flour
1 cup milk
2 eggs
½ teaspoon salt

Place rib roast fat side up on rack in shallow roasting pan. Sprinkle with salt and pepper and insert meat thermometer in thickest part of beef, avoiding fat. Roast uncovered at 325 degrees for about 1¾ hours or to desired degree of doneness: 130 to 135 degrees for rare; 150 to 155 degrees for medium. Shortly before beef is done, prepare Yorkshire pudding by beating all batter ingredients until smooth. Remove beef from oven and transfer to platter; cover with aluminum foil. Heat 9x9-inch pan in oven at 425 degrees. Pour ¼ cup meat drippings, adding vegetable oil if necessary, into heated pan. Add pudding batter and bake for 25 minutes or until puffed and golden brown. Cut into squares and serve with sliced roast beef.

Sweet-and-Sour Chops

4 loin-cut pork chops,
  excess fat trimmed

4 medium potatoes,
  cut into ¾-inch slices

2 (10.5 ounce) cans condensed
  cream of mushroom soup

1 small onion, diced

1 garlic clove, minced

3 tablespoons honey

3 tablespoons prepared mustard

3 tablespoons lemon juice

½ teaspoon Worcestershire sauce

½ teaspoon parsley flakes

½ teaspoon sage

½ teaspoon thyme

Salt and pepper to taste

In large skillet, quickly brown pork chops on both sides. Place pork chops in large baking dish and set aside. Boil potatoes in salted water until slightly softened. Drain well and layer over pork chops. In large bowl, combine remaining ingredients; stir until thoroughly combined. Pour mixture over potatoes and chops. Bake at 350 degrees for 25 to 30 minutes or until pork chops are done. YIELD: 4 SERVINGS.

Orange Duck

½ cup orange juice
½ cup apple jelly
Dash pepper
1 (5 pound) dressed duck
Salt and pepper to taste
1 large stalk celery,
  cut into 2-inch pieces

1 small onion, quartered
⅔ cup long-grain rice, uncooked
1 (12.75 ounce) package instant
  wild rice
⅓ cup chopped fresh parsley

Combine orange juice, jelly, and pepper in small saucepan. Cook over medium heat until jelly melts and mixture bubbles, stirring frequently. Remove from heat and keep warm. Rub cavity of duck with salt and pepper; place celery and onion pieces in cavity. Place duck, breast side up, on rack in roasting pan. Baste lightly with melted jelly mixture. Bake uncovered at 375 degrees for 1 hour, basting frequently with jelly mixture. If duck starts to brown too much, cover loosely with aluminum foil. Bake for another 1 to 1½ hours or until meat thermometer reads 185 degrees when placed in thickest part of duck breast, basting frequently. Prepare long-grain rice and wild rice according to package directions. Combine cooked rice and parsley; stir well. Spoon onto serving platter. Place duck on top of rice. YIELD: 4 SERVINGS.

Oriental Charcoal-Broiled Roast

5 ounces soy sauce
2 cups tomato juice
Juice of 2 lemons

1 tablespoon dried minced onion
2 to 3 pounds chuck roast, cut
  about 2 inches thick

Combine soy sauce, tomato juice, lemon juice, and onion to make marinade. Marinate roast for several hours or overnight. Grill over hot charcoals; cut into thin slices to serve. YIELD: 6 SERVINGS.

Pheasant with Wild Rice Stuffing

3 pounds cleaned pheasant
2 tablespoons butter
¾ cup diced celery
¼ cup diced onion
1 cup thinly sliced mushrooms
1 teaspoon salt
¼ teaspoon pepper
1 tablespoon parsley flakes
½ teaspoon rosemary
1½ cups cooked wild rice
3 bacon slices

Rinse pheasant; pat dry. Melt butter in skillet. Add celery, onion, and mushrooms. Sauté until vegetables are tender and translucent. Remove from heat. Add remaining ingredients, except bacon, tossing with fork. Spoon stuffing into cavity of bird and truss by tying a piece of string to end of neck skin and pulling it over back. Slip ends of wings over back and press them close to body. Press thighs close to body and draw ends of string back on each side and up over thighs. Cross string between legs and tie down under tail. Place bird on rack in shallow roasting pan. Lay bacon slices over top breast. Roast at 325 degrees for 2 hours, basting occasionally with pan drippings. Remove string before cutting and serving. YIELD: 3 TO 4 SERVINGS.

Rotisserie-Style Chicken

1 (4 to 5 pound) whole chicken
2 teaspoons salt
1 teaspoon paprika
½ teaspoon onion powder
½ teaspoon thyme
½ teaspoon pepper
½ teaspoon oregano
¼ teaspoon cayenne pepper
¼ teaspoon garlic powder
1 onion, quartered

Remove giblets from chicken. Rinse out chicken cavity and pat dry. Set aside. In small bowl, mix together spices. Rub spice mixture on inside and outside of chicken. Place onion inside chicken cavity. Place chicken in sealable bag and refrigerate overnight. Remove chicken from bag and place in roasting pan. Bake uncovered at 250 degrees for 5 hours or until meat thermometer reads 180 degrees. YIELD: 4 SERVINGS.

Roast Goose with Browned Potatoes

1 (9 to 11 pound) goose
Salt and pepper

4 to 6 large potatoes,
   pared and cut into halves
Paprika

Remove excess fat from goose. Lightly rub salt into cavity of goose. With skewer, fasten neck skin to back. Fold wings across back with tips touching and tie drumsticks to tail. Pierce skin liberally with fork. Place goose breast side up in shallow roasting pan and roast uncovered at 325 degrees for 3 to 3½ hours, removing excess fat from pan occasionally. One hour and 15 minutes before goose is done, place potatoes around goose in roasting pan. Brush potatoes with goose drippings and sprinkle with salt, pepper, and paprika. Place tent of aluminum foil loosely over goose to prevent excessive browning if necessary. After baking, cover and let stand for 15 minutes for easier carving.

Turkey Scaloppini

½ to ¾ pound turkey cutlets
½ cup flour
½ teaspoon salt
¼ teaspoon pepper
¼ teaspoon basil
3 tablespoons butter or margarine, divided

2 tablespoons olive oil
1 garlic clove, minced
¼ pound sliced fresh mushrooms
2 tablespoons lemon juice
⅓ cup chicken broth
¼ cup white wine or additional chicken broth

Between sheets of waxed paper, pound cutlets to ⅛-inch thickness. Combine flour, salt, pepper, and basil. Dredge cutlets in seasoned flour and shake off excess. In skillet, melt 2 tablespoons butter. Add oil and stir in garlic. Brown cutlets until golden, about 3 minutes. Place browned meat in ovenproof casserole. Melt remaining 1 tablespoon butter in skillet; add mushrooms. Sauté until mushrooms have softened; spoon over meat. In same skillet, combine lemon juice with broth and wine. Cook until heated through. Pour over casserole. Bake at 325 degrees for 30 to 35 minutes. YIELD: 4 SERVINGS.

Sides

Almond Rice

1¾ cups water
½ cup orange juice
½ teaspoon salt
1 cup uncooked long-grain rice
2 tablespoons butter or margarine
2 tablespoons brown sugar

½ cup sliced natural almonds
1 teaspoon minced crystallized
 ginger
¼ teaspoon grated orange peel
Additional orange peel (optional)

In medium saucepan, bring water, orange juice, and salt to a boil; gradually add rice, stirring constantly. Cover, reduce heat, and simmer for 20 to 25 minutes or until rice is tender and liquid is absorbed. Meanwhile, melt butter and brown sugar in small skillet over medium heat. Stir in almonds and ginger; sauté for 2 minutes or until almonds are lightly browned. Add almond mixture and grated orange peel to rice; stir gently to combine. Garnish with additional orange peel if desired. YIELD: 4 SERVINGS.

Candy Apple Salad

2 cups water
¼ cup red cinnamon candies
1 (3 ounce) package cherry gelatin

½ cup chopped celery
1½ cups chopped tart apples
½ cup chopped walnuts

In saucepan, bring water to a boil. Add cinnamon candies; stir until dissolved. Remove from heat and add gelatin; stir until dissolved. Cool slightly and refrigerate until gelatin begins to thicken. Add remaining ingredients; blend well. Pour into 8x8-inch dish and chill until firm. YIELD: 6 SERVINGS.

Auntie's Bean Salad

SALAD:
1 (16 ounce) can green beans
1 (16 ounce) can wax beans
1 (16 ounce) can lima beans
1 (16 ounce) can chickpeas
½ cup chopped green pepper
½ cup chopped onion
¼ cup chopped pimento

DRESSING:
½ cup vegetable oil
½ cup white wine vinegar
½ cup sugar
2 teaspoons salt
½ teaspoon white pepper
¼ teaspoon black pepper

Mix salad ingredients together. In separate bowl, blend dressing ingredients well and pour over bean mixture. Toss. Marinate in refrigerator overnight. Serve cold.

Champagne Salad

1 (8 ounce) package cream cheese, softened
¾ cup sugar
1 (20 ounce) can crushed pineapple, drained
1 (10 ounce) package frozen strawberries, with juice, partially thawed

2 bananas, sliced
½ cup chopped nuts
1 (16 ounce) container frozen whipped topping, thawed

Beat cream cheese with sugar. In separate bowl, mix together pineapple, strawberries with juice, bananas, nuts, and whipped topping. Gently combine with cream cheese mixture. Pour into 9x13-inch pan and freeze completely. To serve, thaw slightly and cut into squares. Keep leftovers frozen. YIELD: 12 TO 16 SERVINGS.

Christmas Fruit Salad

3 egg yolks, beaten
3 tablespoons water
3 tablespoons vinegar
½ teaspoon salt
2 cups whipping cream, whipped
3 cups mini marshmallows
2 cups seedless green grapes, halved

1 (20 ounce) can pineapple tidbits, drained
1 (11 ounce) can mandarin oranges, drained
1 (10 ounce) jar red maraschino cherries, drained and sliced
1 cup chopped pecans
3 tablespoons lemon juice

In large saucepan, combine egg yolks, water, vinegar, and salt. Stirring constantly, cook over medium heat until mixture thickens. Remove from heat and fold in whipped cream. In large bowl, mix together remaining ingredients. Add dressing and stir gently to combine. Cover and refrigerate overnight. Yield: 12 to 14 servings.

Cinnamon Sweet Potatoes

2½ pounds sweet potatoes or yams (7 or 8 medium)
½ cup packed brown sugar
¼ cup butter or margarine

3 tablespoons water
½ teaspoon cinnamon
½ teaspoon salt

Heat salted water (½ teaspoon salt to 1 cup water) to boiling. Add sweet potatoes. Cover and bring back to a boil, cooking 30 to 35 minutes or until tender. Drain. Remove skins. Cut potatoes crosswise into ½-inch slices. Combine brown sugar, margarine, water, cinnamon, and salt in 10-inch skillet. Cook over medium heat, stirring constantly until smooth. Add potato slices and stir until glazed and heated through.

Chive Mashed Potatoes

2½ pounds potatoes (about 8 medium), peeled and cut into 1-inch cubes

1 (8 ounce) package cream cheese, cubed and softened

¾ to 1 cup milk

½ cup snipped fresh chives

1¼ teaspoons salt

¼ teaspoon pepper

Boil potatoes in covered medium saucepan in 2 inches water for 10 to 12 minutes or until tender; drain. Return to pan and mash with electric mixer or potato masher, gradually stirring in cream cheese until blended. Blend in milk, chives, salt, and pepper. Stir gently over medium heat until heated through. Serve immediately. YIELD: 8 SERVINGS.

Corn Bread Dressing

4 stalks celery, diced

2 medium onions, diced

¼ cup butter or margarine, melted

6 cups prepared corn bread, crumbled

5 slices day-old bread, wheat or white, crumbled

1 pound bulk pork sausage, cooked and drained

1½ cups finely chopped cooked ham

¾ cup almonds, toasted and chopped

¾ cup chopped fresh parsley

1½ teaspoons pepper

1 teaspoon poultry seasoning

1 teaspoon sage

2 cups chicken broth

1 egg, lightly beaten

Sauté celery and onion in butter until tender. Combine with breads, sausage, ham, almonds, and seasonings in large bowl; toss well. Add broth and egg to corn bread mixture; stir well. If desired, dressing may be baked separately from turkey in lightly greased 9x13-inch baking dish. Bake uncovered at 350 degrees for 45 minutes to 1 hour or until lightly browned. Unstuffed turkey should be baked 5 minutes less per pound than stuffed turkey.

Cauliflower Salad

4 cups cauliflower florets
1 cup stuffed green olives, chopped
⅔ cup chopped green pepper
½ cup chopped onion
½ cup pimento (may include ones in stuffed olives)

½ cup salad oil
3 tablespoons lemon juice
3 tablespoons wine vinegar
1 tablespoon salt
½ teaspoon sugar
¼ teaspoon pepper

Combine cauliflower, olives, green pepper, onion, and pimento. Shake remaining ingredients together to make dressing and pour over vegetables. Chill for 4 hours.

English Pea Casserole

½ cup chopped onion
1 small sweet red pepper, chopped
¼ cup butter or margarine, melted
1 (5 ounce) package medium egg noodles
1 (8 ounce) package cream cheese, softened

2 cups (8 ounces) shredded sharp cheddar cheese
1 (10 ounce) package frozen English peas, thawed and drained
1 (2.5 ounce) jar mushroom stems and pieces, undrained
½ teaspoon pepper
10 butter-flavored crackers, crushed

In small skillet, sauté onion and red pepper in butter until tender. Set aside. Cook noodles according to package directions; drain. Add cream cheese and cheddar cheese to hot noodles; stir until cheeses melt. Stir in onion mixture, peas, mushrooms, and pepper. Spoon into greased baking dish and top with cracker crumbs. Cover and bake at 325 degrees for 25 to 30 minutes. YIELD: 8 SERVINGS.

Creamy Corn Casserole

3 tablespoons butter or margarine, divided

1 cup finely chopped celery

¼ cup finely chopped onion

¼ cup finely chopped red pepper

1 (10.5 ounce) can condensed cream of chicken soup

3 cups fresh, frozen, or canned corn, drained

1 (8 ounce) can sliced water chestnuts, drained

½ cup soft bread crumbs

Melt 2 tablespoons butter in medium skillet. Add celery, onion, and red pepper and sauté until vegetables are tender, about 2 minutes. Remove from heat and stir in soup, corn, and water chestnuts. Spoon into greased 2-quart casserole dish. Toss bread crumbs with remaining 1 tablespoon melted butter. Sprinkle on top of casserole and bake uncovered at 350 degrees for 25 to 30 minutes. YIELD: 8 SERVINGS.

Farmhouse Potato Salad

4 cups hash browns
1 tablespoon salt in 1 quart
  boiling water
¼ cup sour cream
1 teaspoon salt
¼ teaspoon pepper

4 tablespoons diced sweet pickles
½ teaspoon mustard
¼ cup chopped celery
2 tablespoons chopped sweet onion
2 hard-boiled eggs, chopped

Cook hash browns in salted boiling water in large covered saucepan until tender. Drain. Set aside. Combine sour cream, 1 teaspoon salt, pepper, pickles, and mustard; mix until smooth. Add celery, onion, and eggs; stir lightly. Pour over warm potatoes. Toss lightly and cover. Refrigerate for several hours. Serve chilled.

Cranberry Salad

1 (3 ounce) package cherry gelatin
1 cup hot water
1 can whole-berry cranberry sauce
1 cup sour cream
½ cup chopped pecans

Mix gelatin with hot water. Stir until dissolved. Refrigerate until slightly congealed. Stir in cranberry sauce, sour cream, and pecans. Pour into mold and refrigerate until completely set. YIELD: 4 TO 6 SERVINGS.

Cranberry Waldorf Salad

3 (3 ounce) packages peach gelatin
1¼ teaspoons salt
3 cups boiling water
2 cups cranberry juice cocktail
2 tablespoons lemon juice
1½ cups chopped apples
½ cup coarsely chopped nuts

Dissolve gelatin and salt in boiling water. Stir in cranberry juice and lemon juice. Chill until slightly thickened. Fold in apples and nuts. Chill until firm. Salad may be placed in 2-quart mold.

Evergreen Gelatin Salad

1 large package lime gelatin
2 cups boiling water
1 (8 ounce) package cream cheese, softened
1 (15 ounce) can crushed pineapple
1 (12 ounce) container frozen whipped topping, thawed

Combine gelatin and boiling water; allow to cool. Combine cream cheese, pineapple, and whipped topping. Add to gelatin mixture. Chill until firm. YIELD: 12 SERVINGS.

French Rice

1 (10.75 ounce) can condensed
  french onion soup
½ cup butter or margarine, melted
1 (4.5 ounce) jar sliced mushrooms

1 (8 ounce) can sliced water chestnuts
1 cup uncooked long-grain rice

Preheat oven to 350 degrees. In large bowl, combine soup and butter. Drain mushrooms and water chestnuts, reserving liquid. Add enough water to reserved liquid to equal 1⅓ cups. Add liquid, mushrooms, water chestnuts, and rice to soup mixture; stir well. Pour into lightly greased 6x10-inch baking dish. Cover and bake for 1 hour. YIELD: 6 SERVINGS.

French-Style Green Beans

⅔ cup slivered almonds
6 tablespoons butter or margarine

2 (10 ounce) packages frozen
  french-style green beans, thawed
½ teaspoon salt

In large skillet, sauté almonds in butter until lightly browned, about 1 to 2 minutes. Stir in beans and salt; cook and stir for 1 to 2 minutes or until heated through. YIELD: 8 SERVINGS.

Fresh Cranberry Relish

2 large oranges
4 cups fresh cranberries, washed
  and stemmed

2 red apples, cored but not pared
2 cups sugar

Peel oranges and reserve half of 1 peel. Chop oranges coarsely. Put cranberries, apples, and reserved peel through coarse blade of food chopper or food processor. Add oranges and sugar; mix well. Chill for at least 2 hours before serving.

Glazed Carrots

1¼ pounds fresh carrots (about 8 medium)

⅓ cup packed brown sugar

2 tablespoons butter or margarine

½ teaspoon salt

½ teaspoon grated orange peel

Cut carrots in sections 2½ inches in length, then into ⅜-inch strips. Bring 1 inch salted water to a boil. Add carrots, cover, and bring to a boil again. Reduce heat and cook for 18 to 20 minutes or until tender; drain. Combine brown sugar, butter, salt, and orange peel in 10-inch skillet; stir and cook until bubbly. Add carrots and cook over low heat for about 5 minutes or until carrots are glazed and heated through.

Make-Ahead Mashed Potatoes

3 pounds medium-size potatoes,
  peeled
1½ cups sour cream
5 tablespoons butter or margarine,
  divided

1½ teaspoons salt
¼ teaspoon pepper
¼ cup bread crumbs

Cook potatoes to boiling in salted water until tender. Drain well. In large bowl, combine potatoes, sour cream, 4 tablespoons butter, salt, and pepper. Beat at low speed until blended; beat at high speed until light and fluffy. Spoon into lightly greased 2-quart casserole dish. Cover and refrigerate overnight. Bake covered at 325 degrees for 1 hour. Melt remaining 1 tablespoon butter and mix with bread crumbs. Sprinkle over potatoes. Continue baking uncovered for 30 minutes.

Green Peas with Celery and Onion

2 (10 ounce) packages frozen peas
½ cup sliced celery
1 small onion, thinly sliced

3 tablespoons butter or margarine, softened
¼ teaspoon salt

Following directions on package for peas, cook together peas, celery, and onion; drain. Stir in margarine and salt.

Kidney Bean Salad

⅓ cup mayonnaise
1 teaspoon prepared mustard
1 medium sweet onion, finely chopped
1 cup finely chopped celery
1 small cucumber, diced

2 (16 ounce) cans dark red kidney beans, drained and rinsed
4 hard-boiled eggs, cut into 8 pieces each
Seasoned salt
Lettuce
Red and green vegetables

Mix mayonnaise, mustard, onion, celery, and cucumber. Fold in kidney beans and eggs. Season to taste with seasoned salt. Chill for 2 hours to blend flavors. Serve on lettuce and garnish with red and green vegetables for Christmas.

Mandarin Orange Salad

2 cups boiling water
1 (6 ounce) package orange gelatin
1 pint orange sherbet

1 (11 ounce) can mandarin oranges, drained
1 (8.5 ounce) can crushed pineapple, undrained

In mixing bowl, pour boiling water over gelatin. Stir until dissolved. Spoon orange sherbet into gelatin and stir until well combined. Fold in remaining ingredients. Pour into gelatin mold and refrigerate until firm. YIELD: 8 SERVINGS.

Layered Broccoli-Cauliflower Salad

6 slices bacon
1 cup broccoli florets
1 cup cauliflower florets
3 hard-boiled eggs, chopped
½ cup chopped red onion
1 cup mayonnaise
½ cup sugar
2 tablespoons white wine vinegar
1 cup shredded cheddar cheese

In large skillet, cook bacon over medium-high heat until crispy. Crumble and set aside. In medium glass salad bowl, layer in order broccoli, cauliflower, eggs, and onion. Prepare dressing by whisking together mayonnaise, sugar, and vinegar. Drizzle dressing over top. Sprinkle cheese and crumbled bacon over dressing. Chill completely to blend flavors. YIELD: 8 SERVINGS.

Marinated Vegetable Salad

¾ cup vinegar
½ cup vegetable oil
1 cup sugar
1 teaspoon salt
½ teaspoon black pepper
2 (11 ounce) cans white corn
1 (15 ounce) can small sweet peas
1 (15 ounce) can french-style green beans
1 cup diced green pepper
1 cup diced celery
1 cup diced onion
1 (2 ounce) jar diced pimento

In small saucepan, bring vinegar, oil, sugar, salt, and pepper to a boil; stir until sugar dissolves. Cool. Combine remaining ingredients in serving bowl. Stir in vinegar mixture. Chill for 8 hours or overnight. Drain before serving. YIELD: 10 TO 12 SERVINGS.

Marinated Mushroom-Spinach Salad

½ cup vegetable oil
¼ cup white wine vinegar
1 small onion, sliced
½ teaspoon basil
1 teaspoon salt

¾ teaspoon freshly ground
 black pepper
½ pound mushrooms, washed
 and thinly sliced
1 pound spinach, washed and torn
 into bite-size pieces

In medium bowl, combine oil, vinegar, onion, basil, salt, and pepper. Add mushrooms. Let stand at room temperature for 2 hours or refrigerate overnight, stirring occasionally. Place spinach in salad bowl; add mushroom-oil mixture and toss well. Serve at once. YIELD: 6 SERVINGS.

Old-Fashioned Bread Stuffing

½ cup butter

1 cup chopped sweet onion

½ cup chopped celery, with leaves

8 cups bread cubes

2 tablespoons hot chicken or turkey broth

1 teaspoon salt

¼ teaspoon pepper

1 teaspoon sage

½ teaspoon thyme

½ teaspoon marjoram

Melt butter in skillet. Add onion and celery; cook until soft but not browned. Combine butter mixture with bread cubes, broth, and seasonings. For soft, moist dressing, use fresh or slightly stale bread. For lighter, fluffier dressing, use dried, stale bread. Makes enough to stuff an 8- to 10-pound turkey.

Old-Fashioned Mashed Potatoes

8 medium potatoes, peeled
and sliced
1 medium onion, finely chopped
Water
½ to ⅔ cup whole milk, divided
⅓ cup butter

1½ teaspoons grated
parmesan cheese
1 teaspoon salt
¼ teaspoon sugar
Dash pepper

Cook potatoes and onion until tender in enough boiling water to cover. Drain and mash. Add ½ cup milk and remaining ingredients. Mix together. Add more milk, if needed for desired consistency. Serve hot.

Orange-Sweet Potato Casserole

4 large sweet potatoes
½ cup brown sugar, divided
2 tablespoons butter or margarine,
divided
1 (11 ounce) can mandarin oranges,
drained
½ cup orange juice

TOPPING:
½ cup chopped walnuts
¼ cup sweetened, flaked coconut
1 tablespoon brown sugar
½ teaspoon cinnamon
2 tablespoons butter or margarine

Boil whole potatoes for 30 to 40 minutes. Cool; peel and slice into ¼-inch slices. Arrange half of potato slices in greased casserole dish. Sprinkle with ¼ cup brown sugar. Dot with 1 tablespoon butter. Arrange half of oranges on top. Repeat layers. Pour orange juice over all. Cover and bake at 350 degrees for 45 minutes. While casserole is baking, mix together walnuts, coconut, brown sugar, and cinnamon. Cut 2 tablespoons butter into mixture and set aside. Remove casserole from oven, uncover, and sprinkle topping over potatoes. Return to oven uncovered for 10 minutes. YIELD: 8 SERVINGS.

Oyster Corn Bread Dressing

2 (8 ounce) packages corn bread
   mix
4 tablespoons butter
¾ cup chopped onion
3 stalks celery, chopped
2 cloves garlic, minced

2 (8 ounce) cans oysters, liquid
   reserved and oysters chopped
2 eggs, beaten
½ teaspoon pepper
1½ teaspoons sage
3 teaspoons poultry seasoning
1 (14 ounce) can chicken stock

Prepare corn bread as instructed on package; allow to cool before crumbling corn bread into large bowl. In large saucepan, melt butter over low heat and sauté onion, celery, garlic, and oysters until onion is glassy and tender. Stir oyster mixture into corn bread crumbs. In separate bowl, beat eggs; season with pepper, sage, and poultry seasoning. Mix in chicken stock and reserved oyster liquid. Blend egg mixture into corn bread mixture. Transfer to greased 2-quart casserole dish. Bake uncovered at 350 degrees for 45 minutes. YIELD: 8 SERVINGS.

Spinach-Stuffed Tomatoes

1 (10 ounce) package frozen
   chopped spinach
¼ cup water
¼ cup mayonnaise

1 tablespoon dried minced onion
⅛ teaspoon nutmeg
Salt and pepper to taste
6 small whole tomatoes

Cook spinach in water for 3 minutes, stirring to defrost; drain completely. Combine spinach with mayonnaise, minced onion, nutmeg, salt, and pepper. Cut thin slice off tops of tomatoes and scoop out center; drain upside down. Sprinkle inside of tomatoes with salt and fill with spinach mixture. Place tomatoes in baking dish and pour hot water ¼ inch deep around tomatoes. Bake at 350 degrees for 12 to 15 minutes.

Stuffed Winter Squash

3 small acorn or butternut squash
1 large sweet onion, diced
1 tablespoon olive oil
1 cup finely diced celery
1 cup coarsely chopped
  fresh spinach

1 cup whole wheat bread crumbs
¼ teaspoon salt
¼ cup finely ground almonds
2 tablespoons butter

Clean squash and cut each in half, removing seeds. Bake at 350 degrees for 35 minutes or until tender. Sauté onions in oil until soft. Add diced celery. Cover and simmer on medium heat until tender. Add spinach; stir to wilt. Combine bread crumbs with salt and ground almonds. Stuff squash halves with spinach mixture and sprinkle crumb mixture on top. Dot with butter. Return to oven for 10 to 15 minutes.

Willett's Broccoli-Rice Tradition

1 cup chopped onion

2 tablespoons butter

1 (10.5 ounce) can condensed cream of chicken or mushroom soup

1 teaspoon salt

½ teaspoon freshly ground black pepper

3 cups cooked rice

1 (10 ounce) package frozen chopped broccoli, thawed

2 cups shredded cheddar cheese

In large skillet, cook onions in butter until tender crisp. Add soup, salt, and pepper. Add remaining ingredients, mixing well; transfer to buttered 2-quart baking dish. Bake at 350 degrees for 35 minutes or until hot and bubbly.

Mixed Vegetable Medley

1 (10 ounce) package frozen peas
1 (10 ounce) package frozen
  green beans
1 (10 ounce) package frozen
  cauliflower
¾ cup water

1 (2 ounce) jar diced
  pimento, drained
2 tablespoons butter or margarine
½ teaspoon basil
½ teaspoon salt
⅛ teaspoon pepper

Bring vegetables and water to a boil and reduce heat. Cover and cook over low heat for about 7 minutes or until vegetables are tender. Drain and stir in remaining ingredients. YIELD: 10 TO 12 SERVINGS.

Sweet Potato Casserole

2 large sweet potatoes
3 eggs, beaten
¼ cup butter, melted
⅔ cup evaporated milk

TOPPING:
1 cup chopped pecans
½ cup brown sugar
¼ cup flour
2 tablespoons butter, melted

Wash, peel, and cut sweet potatoes. Boil for about 25 minutes or until tender. Drain well and mash. Stir in eggs, butter, and evaporated milk. Spoon into baking dish. Combine topping ingredients and sprinkle evenly over sweet potatoes. Bake at 350 degrees for 40 minutes or until set.

Wilted Spinach Salad

8 slices bacon, diced
1 tablespoon brown sugar
⅓ cup thinly sliced green onions
Salt to taste
3 tablespoons vinegar

¼ teaspoon dry mustard
1 pound fresh spinach, washed, dried, and chilled
1 hard-boiled egg, chopped

In heavy skillet, fry diced bacon until crisp; reduce heat. Stir in brown sugar, onions, salt, vinegar, and mustard; bring to a boil. Pour hot mixture over spinach. Toss lightly. Sprinkle chopped egg over salad. Serve immediately.
YIELD: 6 SERVINGS.

Zesty Carrots

6 to 8 carrots, cut into ¼-inch slices
½ cup mayonnaise
2 tablespoons dried minced onion
1 tablespoon prepared horseradish
¼ cup shredded cheddar cheese

1 teaspoon salt
¼ teaspoon pepper
½ cup crushed cornflakes
1 tablespoon butter or margarine, melted

Place carrots in saucepan and cover with water. Cook for 5 minutes. Drain, reserving ¼ cup water. Pour reserved liquid into mixing bowl. Stir in mayonnaise, minced onion, horseradish, cheese, salt, and pepper. Mix well. Add carrots. Transfer to greased 2-quart casserole dish. Sprinkle with crushed cornflakes and drizzle with butter. Bake at 350 degrees for 20 to 25 minutes.
YIELD: 8 SERVINGS.

Christmas Eve
CELEBRATIONS

Expectancy is the atmosphere for miracles.
EDWIN LOUIS COLE

Lord, we long to celebrate Your birth in myriad ways. Bless us as we feast and rejoice with full hearts this Christmas season. Come among us and inspire our worship as only You can do! Amen.

The house of Israel named it manna, and it was like coriander seed, white, and its taste was like wafers with honey.

EXODUS 16:31 NASB

Bierock Casserole

2 pounds lean ground beef
1 medium onion, diced
1 small head cabbage, chopped

Salt and pepper to taste
1 (36 count) package frozen rolls

In large skillet, brown meat with diced onion. Add cabbage; cover and cook until cabbage is tender. Add salt and pepper to taste. Grease two 9x13-inch baking pans. Place 18 rolls in each pan. Let rise. Press down gently. Spoon cabbage mixture on top of rolls in one pan. Flip rolls from other pan over top of cabbage. Press down lightly. Bake at 350 degrees for 30 to 35 minutes or until rolls are browned. YIELD: 9 SERVINGS.

Broiled Shrimp

1 cup butter
2 cloves garlic, minced
¼ cup lemon juice
½ teaspoon salt
¼ teaspoon freshly ground
    black pepper

2 pounds large shrimp, peeled and
    deveined
Chopped fresh parsley

In saucepan over low heat, melt butter with garlic, but don't allow garlic to scorch. Remove from heat and add lemon juice, salt, and pepper. Place shrimp in shallow baking dish and pour sauce over shrimp. Broil shrimp 4 to 5 inches from heating element for 6 to 8 minutes. Turn and baste shrimp halfway through. When done, shrimp should be pink and tender. Garnish with chopped fresh parsley. YIELD: 6 SERVINGS.

Cheddar Chowder

3 cups water
1 teaspoon salt
¼ teaspoon pepper
4 cups diced potatoes
1 cup sliced carrots
1 cup sliced celery

½ cup chopped onion
¼ cup margarine
¼ cup flour
2 cups milk
2 cups shredded cheddar cheese
2 cups cubed cooked ham

Add water, salt, and pepper to soup pot. Add potatoes, carrots, celery, and onion. Bring to a boil; reduce heat and simmer until vegetables are tender. Do not drain. In medium saucepan over low heat, make white sauce with margarine, flour, and milk. Add cheese and stir until melted. Add ham and cheese sauce to soup mixture. Heat; do not boil. Remove from stove. Soup will thicken as it cools.

Cheesy Broccoli Chowder

1½ pounds fresh broccoli or 2 (10 ounce) packages frozen broccoli
1 (12.5 ounce) can chicken broth
2 (10.5 ounce) cans condensed cream of mushroom soup

2 cups milk
1 cup light cream
¾ pound swiss cheese, grated
Croutons

Cook broccoli in chicken broth until tender. Add remaining ingredients except swiss cheese and croutons. Simmer for 30 minutes, stirring occasionally. Before serving, add cheese to soup. Stir until cheese melts; serve topped with croutons.

Corn Chowder

5 slices bacon, cooked, drippings reserved

1 (1 pound) can whole kernel corn, drained, liquid reserved

1 medium onion, diced

1 cup diced potato

½ teaspoon salt

1 (10.5 ounce) can condensed cream of celery soup

½ cup milk

Drain bacon on paper towels and crumble; set aside. To bacon drippings, add corn liquid, onion, potatoes, and salt. Cover and simmer for 15 minutes or until potatoes are tender. Add soup, milk, corn, and bacon. Heat through.

Cream of Zucchini Soup

4 medium zucchini, quartered and sliced

4 cups chicken broth

8 green onions, chopped

Salt and pepper to taste

½ teaspoon dill weed

2 (8 ounce) packages cream cheese, softened

1 cup sour cream

Chives and paprika for garnish

In saucepan, combine zucchini, chicken broth, green onions, salt, pepper, and dill weed. Cook for 20 minutes or until soft. In blender, process cream cheese and sour cream until smooth. Add cooled zucchini mixture, 1 cup at a time, blending until smooth. Pour into large bowl and refrigerate overnight or until very cold. Serve warm or cold with garnish of chives and paprika. YIELD: 8 SERVINGS.

Curried Butternut Squash Soup

¼ cup butter or margarine
2 cups chopped onion
4 teaspoons curry powder
3 pounds butternut squash, peeled, seeded, and diced

2 apples, peeled, cored, and chopped
4 cups chicken broth
Salt and pepper to taste
Seasoned croutons

In large soup pot, melt butter. Add onion and curry powder; sauté for 15 minutes or until onion is soft. Add squash, apples, and chicken broth; cover and simmer for 25 minutes or until squash is tender. Puree soup in blender, about 2 cups at a time. Return soup to pot and season with salt and pepper. Serve hot with croutons. YIELD: 10 CUPS.

Herb Potato Soup

8 medium potatoes
1 teaspoon dried minced onion
4 tablespoons butter
2 tablespoons chopped fresh parsley
1 teaspoon dried basil
6 tablespoons flour

2 teaspoons salt
½ teaspoon pepper
2 cups chicken stock
2 cups milk
4 cups half-and-half

Cook potatoes and minced onion until potatoes are soft. Drain and reserve 2 cups potato water. Grate potatoes and set aside. Melt butter in large soup pot and add seasonings. Gradually add reserved potato water and last 3 ingredients. Cook over medium heat, stirring constantly, until mixture thickens slightly. Add grated potatoes and heat on low.

Hot Seafood Salad

3 tablespoons chopped green pepper
3 tablespoons chopped onion
1 cup chopped celery
1 cup mayonnaise
1 cup flaked crabmeat
1 cup cooked shrimp
1 teaspoon salt
1 teaspoon pepper
1 teaspoon Worcestershire sauce
1 cup crushed potato chips

In mixing bowl, combine all ingredients except chips. Transfer to 8x8-inch pan. Top with chips and bake at 350 degrees for 25 to 30 minutes.

Lamb Stew

1 pound lamb, cut into ¾-inch pieces
2 tablespoons olive oil
3 cups beef broth
3 cloves garlic, minced
1 teaspoon marjoram
1 bay leaf
¼ teaspoon salt
¼ teaspoon pepper
2 large potatoes, peeled and cut into ½-inch chunks
1½ cups sliced carrots
1½ cups chopped celery
½ cup chopped onion
½ cup sour cream
3 tablespoons flour

In large soup pot, brown meat in oil; drain excess fat. Add broth, garlic, marjoram, bay leaf, salt, and pepper and bring to a boil. Reduce heat, cover, and simmer for 20 minutes or until meat is rather tender. Add potatoes, carrots, celery, and onion. Return to a boil and then reduce heat; cover and simmer for 30 minutes or until vegetables are tender. Remove bay leaf. In small bowl, blend sour cream and flour, then stir in ½ cup of liquid from stew. Add sour cream mixture to stew and cook until thickened.

Herbed Salmon Steaks

2 tablespoons butter or margarine
2 tablespoons lemon juice
4 salmon steaks, ¾ inch thick
1 teaspoon onion salt
¼ teaspoon pepper

½ teaspoon marjoram or thyme
Paprika
Lemon wedges and parsley for
  garnish

Place butter and lemon juice in 9x13-inch baking dish and heat in 400-degree oven. Coat both sides of fish with lemon butter mixture and arrange in baking dish. Sprinkle with salt, pepper, and marjoram or thyme. Bake uncovered for about 25 minutes or until fish flakes easily with fork. Sprinkle with paprika and serve with lemon wedges and parsley. YIELD: 4 SERVINGS.

Nana's Baked Beans

1 pound dry navy beans
6 cups cold water
1 teaspoon salt
12 slices bacon

½ cup brown sugar
¼ cup molasses
1 medium onion, chopped
2 teaspoons dry mustard

Rinse beans. Combine beans and water in large saucepan or dutch oven. Cover and bring to a boil; boil for 2 minutes. Remove from heat; let stand for 1 hour or overnight. Add salt. Simmer partially covered for 1 hour or until beans are tender. Drain, reserving liquid. Cut bacon into 1-inch pieces. Combine uncooked bacon, brown sugar, molasses, onion, and dry mustard with beans in dutch oven or 2-quart bean pot. Add 1¾ cups reserved liquid. Bake uncovered at 300 degrees for 5 hours. Add additional water if necessary.

Shrimp Newburg

6 tablespoons butter
2 tablespoons flour
1½ cups light cream
3 egg yolks, beaten
2 cups cooked shrimp
2 teaspoons lemon juice

3 tablespoons water or chicken broth
¼ teaspoon salt
Paprika to taste
Toast points

In saucepan, blend butter and flour; add cream all at once. Heat over low heat and stir until thickened. Stir small amount of hot mixture into yolks; add yolks to mixture in saucepan. Cook, stirring until thick. Add shrimp; then add lemon juice, water or broth, salt, and paprika. Serve with toast points.

Peanut Butter Soup

1 cup peanut butter
3 cups milk, divided
½ cup chopped celery
1½ cups water

1 potato, grated
2 teaspoons salt
½ teaspoon pepper

In mixing bowl, mix peanut butter with 1 cup milk; heat remaining 2 cups milk in double boiler. In large saucepan, cook celery in water until tender. Add grated potato and cook, stirring until mixture thickens. Add hot milk to cooked vegetables. Blend in peanut butter mixture, salt, and pepper. Beat with mixer to cream soup. Serve hot.

Creamy Tomato Soup

2 (16 ounce) cans tomato sauce
1 teaspoon salt
½ teaspoon pepper
1 teaspoon parsley flakes
1 teaspoon celery salt
½ teaspoon cumin
1 cup half-and-half

In large soup pot, combine all ingredients except half-and-half. Simmer on low for 1 hour. Stir in half-and-half and reheat, but do not boil. Yield: 4 servings.

Shrimp with Pasta

16 ounces vermicelli
Salt and pepper to taste
½ cup butter
½ cup olive oil
4 cloves garlic, minced
24 large shrimp, peeled and deveined
8 large fresh mushrooms, sliced
1 cup chopped fresh parsley
Romano cheese

Cook vermicelli in boiling water for 10 minutes. Drain and rinse in cold water. Toss noodles with salt and pepper and set aside. In large skillet, heat butter and oil. Add garlic, shrimp, and mushrooms. Cook until shrimp turns pink, about 5 minutes. Toss in vermicelli and heat through. Transfer to warmed platter and sprinkle with parsley and cheese. Yield: 4 servings.

COOKIES
and
CANDY

Christmas, my child, is love in action.
Every time we love, every time we give, it's Christmas.
DALE EVANS

How amazing, Father, is the sweet fellowship we
enjoy with You, the God of the universe! You came
to us, became one of us, so that we live in the peace,
assurance, and gladness of knowing You as our
Savior and Lord. Thank You! Amen.

*How sweet your words taste to me;
they are sweeter than honey.*

PSALM 119:103 NLT

Cookies

Angel Cookies

1 box angel food cake mix
½ cup water

1 (8 to 12 ounce) bag dried mixed fruit, finely chopped

In mixing bowl, combine cake mix and water. Stir in fruit. Line baking sheet with foil. Drop dough by teaspoons. Bake at 400 degrees for 8 to 10 minutes until puffy and golden in color. Cool well before removing from foil.

Buttermilk Cookies

3½ cups flour
1 teaspoon salt
1 teaspoon baking soda
1 teaspoon baking powder
1 cup butter or margarine, softened

2 cups sugar
2 eggs
1 cup buttermilk
Milk
Colored sugar

In medium bowl, blend flour, salt, baking soda, and baking powder; set aside. In large bowl, cream butter and sugar. Add eggs and beat well. In small amounts, mix in dry ingredients, alternating with buttermilk. Cover and chill dough for at least 2 hours. Drop by teaspoons onto greased baking sheet. Dip bottom of drinking glass into milk and slightly flatten each cookie. Sprinkle with colored sugar. Bake at 350 degrees for 8 to 10 minutes.

Apricot Balls

1 (8 ounce) package dried apricots, finely diced
2½ cups sweetened flaked coconut
¾ cup sweetened condensed milk
1 cup finely chopped nuts (pecans work especially well)

Mix together apricots, coconut, and milk. Shape into 1-inch balls and roll in nuts. Refrigerate. YIELD: 1½ DOZEN.

As a Gift: These rich, festive cookies will look pretty presented in a candy dish or interesting serving bowl you are gifting. Bundle in cellophane wrap and add a bow.

Candy Cane Cookies

1 cup shortening
1 cup powdered sugar
1 egg
1½ teaspoons almond extract
1 teaspoon vanilla
2½ cups flour
1 teaspoon salt
¼ teaspoon baking soda
Red food coloring
6 large candy canes, crushed
Sugar

Mix shortening, powdered sugar, egg, almond flavoring, and vanilla thoroughly. Add flour, salt, and baking soda. Divide dough in half and blend red food coloring into one half. Roll out each half separately and cut into 4-inch strips. For each cookie, twist red and white strips together (candy cane style) and shape like a candy cane. Bake at 350 degrees for 10 minutes. While still hot, sprinkle with mixture of crushed candy canes and sugar.

As a Gift: Arrange 2 to 4 candy cane cookies in a shallow clear plastic box lined with tissue.

Butterfinger Cookies

¾ cup sugar
½ cup butter, softened
1 large egg
1¾ cups flour
¾ teaspoon baking soda

¼ teaspoon salt
1 cup (about three 2.1-ounce bars) Butterfinger candy bars, coarsely chopped

Beat sugar and butter in large bowl until creamy. Beat in egg. In separate bowl, combine flour, baking soda, and salt; gradually beat into egg mixture. Stir in Butterfinger pieces. Drop by slightly rounded tablespoons onto ungreased baking sheet. Bake at 375 degrees for 10 to 12 minutes or until lightly browned. Cool on baking sheet for 2 minutes before removing.

Chocolate Drop Cookies

½ cup shortening
2 squares unsweetened baking
   chocolate
2 eggs

1 cup sugar
½ teaspoon vanilla
1⅓ cups flour

Melt shortening and chocolate together in medium saucepan. Remove from heat. In mixing bowl, beat eggs; add sugar and whisk together well. Add melted chocolate mixture, vanilla, and flour. Mix well. Drop by heaping tablespoons onto ungreased baking sheet. Bake at 400 degrees for 6 minutes.

Chocolate Caramel Cookies

3 cups flour
½ cup cocoa
3 sticks salted butter, softened
1 cup sugar
1 egg
1 teaspoon vanilla
1 (12 ounce) package semisweet
   chocolate chips

1 cup finely chopped pecans,
   toasted
1 (14 ounce) bottle caramel
   ice-cream topping

CHOCOLATE DRIZZLE:
½ cup semisweet chocolate chips
2 teaspoons shortening

In mixing bowl, whisk together flour and cocoa; set aside. In separate bowl, cream together butter and sugar. Beat in egg and vanilla. Gradually add flour mixture. Stir in chocolate chips and pecans. Roll dough into 1-inch balls and place on ungreased baking sheet. Press thumb in center of each ball. Fill each imprint half full with caramel topping. Bake at 350 degrees for 15 to 18 minutes. Cool for 5 minutes before removing from baking sheet. To prepare chocolate drizzle, combine chocolate chips and shortening in microwave-safe bowl and microwave for 30 seconds to 1 minute or until melted. Stir until smooth. With fork, drizzle chocolate over cookies. YIELD: ABOUT 5 DOZEN.

Chocolate Snowballs

1¼ cups butter
⅔ cup sugar
1 teaspoon vanilla
2 cups flour

⅛ teaspoon salt
½ cup cocoa
2 cups chopped pecans
½ cup powdered sugar

In medium bowl, cream butter and sugar until light and fluffy. Stir in vanilla. Sift flour, salt, and cocoa into separate bowl; stir into creamed mixture. Mix in pecans until well blended. Cover dough and chill for at least 2 hours. Roll chilled dough into 1-inch balls. Place on ungreased baking sheet about 2 inches apart. Bake at 350 degrees for 20 minutes. Roll in powdered sugar when cooled.

Chocolate Holiday Cookies

⅔ cup powdered sugar
½ cup butter or margarine, softened
½ teaspoon vanilla

1 cup flour
2 tablespoons cocoa
⅛ teaspoon salt

In mixing bowl, beat together powdered sugar, butter, and vanilla at medium speed. Reduce speed and add flour, cocoa, and salt. Divide dough in half, refrigerating second half until ready to use. Using one half at a time, place dough between sheets of lightly floured waxed paper and roll out to ⅛-inch thickness. Remove top piece of waxed paper and cut dough with 2- to 2½-inch cookie cutters. Place on ungreased baking sheet. Bake at 325 degrees for 14 to 18 minutes. Repeat with second half of dough. Cool cookies completely before decorating with icing (recipe follows) as desired. YIELD: ABOUT 2 DOZEN.

ICING:

1¼ cups powdered sugar
1 tablespoon meringue powder

2 tablespoons warm water
¼ teaspoon cream of tartar

In mixing bowl, combine all icing ingredients and beat at low speed just until moistened. Increase speed and beat until mixture is stiff and glossy. Add more warm water if icing becomes too stiff. Cover with damp paper towel until ready to use.

Cookies in a Jiffy

1 (9 ounce) box yellow cake mix
⅔ cup quick-cooking oats
½ cup butter or margarine, melted

1 egg
½ cup M&M's or butterscotch chips

In mixing bowl, combine first 4 ingredients and beat well. Stir in M&M's or butterscotch chips. Drop by tablespoons 2 inches apart onto ungreased baking sheet. Bake at 350 degrees for 10 to 12 minutes or until lightly browned. Immediately remove cookies to wire racks to cool. YIELD: 2 DOZEN.

Cowboy Cookies

2 cups flour
1 teaspoon baking soda
½ teaspoon baking powder
½ teaspoon salt
1 cup shortening
1 cup sugar

1 cup brown sugar
2 eggs
2 cups old-fashioned rolled oats
1 teaspoon vanilla
1 cup semisweet chocolate chips

In mixing bowl, sift together flour, baking soda, baking powder, and salt. Set aside. Cream together shortening and sugars. Add eggs and beat until light and fluffy. Add flour mixture and mix well. Add rolled oats, vanilla, and chocolate chips. Drop by teaspoons onto greased baking sheet. Bake at 350 degrees for 15 minutes.

Christmas Bells

1 cup butter
½ cup sugar
1 egg
½ teaspoon almond extract
2½ cups flour

FROSTING:
¼ cup butter
2 to 3 cups powdered sugar
½ teaspoon almond extract
Milk, as needed

Cream together butter and sugar. Add egg and extract. Add flour all at once and blend, but don't overmix. Chill for 1 hour. Roll out to ½-inch thickness and cut out with bell cookie cutter. Place on lightly greased baking sheet and bake at 350 degrees for 10 to 12 minutes. To make frosting, combine butter, powdered sugar, and extract. Blend together, adding milk 1 tablespoon at a time until frosting reaches spreadable consistency. YIELD: 2 DOZEN COOKIES.

As a Gift: Present your bell cookies stacked like crackers in a disposable Christmas food box. Tie the cutter into the ribbon as a gift.

Christmas Hands

1 cup shortening
2 cups sugar
2 eggs
½ cup milk
5 cups flour
1 teaspoon baking soda
1 teaspoon baking powder
½ teaspoon salt
1 teaspoon lemon flavoring
1 (16 ounce) can buttercream frosting
Assorted sprinkles and candies for decorating

Cream together shortening and sugar. Add eggs and milk. Mix well. Combine flour, baking soda, baking powder, salt, and lemon flavoring. Blend into creamed mixture. Roll one-fourth of dough at a time, as gently as possible, to ¼-inch thickness. Cut around your children's hand shapes. Place on greased baking sheet and bake at 350 degrees for 8 to 10 minutes. Cool. Frost with buttercream frosting and decorate. YIELD: 4 DOZEN COOKIES.

As a Gift: A very fun and unique treat for grandparents, teachers, aunts, uncles, and cousins! Let your kids decorate them with their names included. Wrap each hand cookie individually in a plastic bag and tie the top with a ribbon.

Old-Fashioned Preserve Thumbprints

1 (8 ounce) package cream cheese, softened
¾ cup butter, softened
1 cup powdered sugar
2¼ cups flour
½ teaspoon baking soda
½ cup chopped pecans
½ teaspoon vanilla
Strawberry and peach preserves

In large bowl, beat cream cheese, butter, and powdered sugar until smooth. Add flour and baking soda, stirring to blend well. Add pecans and vanilla; mix well. Cover and chill for at least 30 minutes. Shape into 1-inch balls and place on ungreased baking sheet. Press thumb in middle of each cookie; fill imprint with about 1 teaspoon preserves. Bake for 14 to 16 minutes or until light golden brown. Cool on wire rack. YIELD: ABOUT 3 DOZEN COOKIES.

Christmas M&M Cookies

1 cup shortening
½ cup sugar
1 cup packed brown sugar
2 eggs
2 teaspoons vanilla

2¼ cups flour
1 teaspoon baking soda
¾ teaspoon salt
2 cups Christmas M&M's

Cream together shortening, sugars, eggs, and vanilla. Combine flour, baking soda, and salt. Stir into creamed mixture. Add M&M's. Mix and bake at 350 degrees for 10 to 12 minutes. YIELD: 3 DOZEN.

As a Gift: Present cookies in a parchment-lined sewing basket you are gifting. Nestle cookies in colorful tissue paper and top with another sheet of parchment to keep from staining the basket lid.

Christmas Tea Cookies

½ cup shortening
¼ cup butter
½ cup powdered sugar
1½ cups flour

¼ teaspoon salt
2 eggs, beaten
1 teaspoon vanilla
¼ cup chopped nuts (optional)

Cream together shortening, butter, and powdered sugar. Combine flour and salt and gently blend into creamed mixture. Don't overmix. Add beaten eggs and vanilla. Add nuts. Chill dough for 2 hours. Shape into balls and roll in powdered sugar. Place on baking sheet and flatten gently. Bake at 350 degrees for 20 minutes. YIELD: 2 DOZEN COOKIES.

As a Gift: Present these cookies in a small, clear bag tied with ribbon, 2 or 3 cookies per bag. Place the bag in a teacup and saucer you are gifting. Insert a couple of wrapped tea bags in with the cookies. Bundle it all in cellophane wrap and tie with a ribbon.

French Christmas Cookies

½ cup butter or shortening,
  softened
¾ cup sugar
½ cup honey

2 egg yolks
¼ cup milk
1 teaspoon vanilla
3 cups flour, sifted

In mixing bowl, cream together butter and sugar until light and fluffy. Stir in honey and egg yolks, beating well. Add milk and vanilla, blending well. Add flour in small amounts, stirring well after each addition. Chill dough for 2 hours. Roll out to ⅛-inch thickness on lightly floured board. Cut into desired shapes and place on ungreased baking sheet. Bake at 375 degrees for 10 minutes. Cool; frost if desired. YIELD: 3 DOZEN.

Grapefruit Sugar Cookies

½ cup shortening
½ cup butter
1 cup sugar
2 eggs
2½ cups flour

2 teaspoons baking powder
½ teaspoon salt
¾ cup candied grapefruit peel,
  finely chopped

Cream together shortening, butter, sugar, and eggs. Combine flour, baking powder, salt, and grapefruit peel. Blend into creamed mixture. Roll to ¼-inch thickness on floured board. Cut into squares or circles. Place on greased baking sheet and bake at 350 degrees for 10 minutes. YIELD: 3 DOZEN COOKIES.

As a Gift: Locate a nice bag of Florida or California grapefruit and present it along with a plate of these delicious and unusual cookies.

Cinnamon Nut Cookies

1 cup shortening
1 cup sugar
4 eggs
1 teaspoon vanilla
4 cups flour

1 teaspoon baking powder
½ teaspoon salt
1 cup chopped pecans
Cinnamon sugar
Red cinnamon candies

Cream together shortening and sugar. Add eggs and vanilla. Combine flour, baking powder, and salt. Blend into creamed mixture. Add nuts. Chill in refrigerator for several hours. Form dough into 2 or 3 long rolls and place on greased baking sheet. Bake at 350 degrees for about 30 minutes. While rolls are still warm, slice into ½-inch slices. Place on baking sheet and sprinkle with cinnamon sugar. Place a red cinnamon candy in center of each cookie and bake for another 10 minutes. YIELD: 4 DOZEN COOKIES.

As a Gift: Arrange these spicy treats in the plastic wrap–lined well of a new nut bowl you're gifting. Bundle in clear gift wrap. Include a small bag of un-shelled mixed nuts.

Pecan Tassies

½ cup butter
1 (3 ounce) package cream cheese
1 cup flour

FILLING:
¾ cup brown sugar

1 egg, beaten
1 tablespoon butter, melted
1 teaspoon vanilla
Pinch salt
¾ to 1 cup chopped pecans

In small bowl, cream together butter and cream cheese; mix in flour. Chill for 1 hour. Form into 24 small balls and press into mini muffin tins; set aside. In small bowl, combine all filling ingredients and spoon filling into cookie shells. Bake at 350 degrees for 25 minutes. YIELD: 2 DOZEN COOKIES.

French Lace

1 cup flour
1 cup finely chopped walnuts
½ cup light corn syrup

½ cup shortening
⅔ cup packed brown sugar

Blend flour and walnuts. Bring corn syrup, shortening, and brown sugar to a boil over medium heat, stirring constantly. Remove from heat and gradually add flour mixture. Drop by teaspoons 3 inches apart on lightly greased baking sheet. Bake just a few cookies at a time at 375 degrees for 5 to 6 minutes. Allow to cool for 5 minutes before removing from baking sheet. YIELD: 1 DOZEN COOKIES.

As a Gift: These delicate, lacy cookies will look pretty in a short stack of 4 or 5, wrapped in Christmas kitchen wrap and topped with a bow.

Holiday Fruit Drops

1 cup shortening
2 cups packed brown sugar
2 eggs
½ cup sour milk
3½ cups flour
1 teaspoon baking soda

1 teaspoon salt
2 cups candied cherries, halved or chopped
2 cups chopped dates
1½ cups pecan halves, divided

Cream shortening and brown sugar. Add eggs. Stir in sour milk. Combine flour, baking soda, and salt. Blend into creamed mixture. Stir in cherries, dates, and half of pecans. Chill for 1 hour. Drop by rounded teaspoons onto lightly greased baking sheet. Place pecan half on each cookie and bake at 400 degrees for 8 to 10 minutes. (These cookies actually *improve* with storage.) YIELD: 3 DOZEN COOKIES.

As a Gift: Present these cookies in a tin reminiscent of old fruitcake containers. Scout antique and secondhand shops for interesting container ideas. A really nice alternative to fruit*cake*!

Old-Fashioned Molasses Cookies

3 cups flour
2 teaspoons baking soda
1 teaspoon salt
1 teaspoon ginger
1 teaspoon cinnamon
¾ cup evaporated milk

¾ tablespoon cider vinegar
1 cup shortening
1 cup sugar
1 egg
½ cup molasses

In medium bowl, stir together flour, baking soda, salt, and spices. In small bowl, combine evaporated milk and vinegar. In large bowl, cream shortening and sugar thoroughly. Add egg and molasses. Beat well. Add milk mixture alternately with flour mixture. Mix well. Drop by teaspoons onto greased baking sheet. Bake at 375 degrees for 10 minutes. Do not overbake. YIELD: 4 DOZEN COOKIES.

As a Gift: Line cookies on end like dominoes in shallow cardboard gift box. These come plain or decorated in cooking and hobby stores. Bundle all in cellophane and tie the top with a bow.

Jam Thumbprints

1 (8 ounce) package cream cheese, softened
¾ cup butter, softened
1 cup powdered sugar
2¼ cups flour
½ teaspoon baking soda
½ cup chopped pecans
½ teaspoon vanilla
Jam or fruit preserves

Beat cream cheese, butter, and powdered sugar until smooth. Add flour and baking soda. Mix well. Add pecans and vanilla. Chill dough for 30 minutes. Shape dough into 1-inch balls and place on ungreased baking sheet. Press thumb in middle of each cookie; fill imprint with about 1 teaspoon of your favorite jam or fruit preserves. Bake at 350 degrees for 14 to 16 minutes. YIELD: 3 DOZEN COOKIES.

As a Gift: Present these delicious cookies on a plastic Christmas plate, bundle in cellophane, and tie a new pair of winter gloves or mittens into the bow.

Italian Christmas Cookies

½ cup butter
½ cup shortening
1 cup sugar
5 eggs
1 teaspoon vanilla
5 cups flour
3 teaspoons baking powder
½ teaspoon salt

FILLING:
1 cup sweetened applesauce or
   apple butter
½ cup crushed walnuts

CHOCOLATE:
1 cup semisweet chocolate chips
1 tablespoon butter

Cream together butter, shortening, and sugar. Stir in eggs and vanilla. Combine flour, baking powder, and salt. Add to creamed mixture and mix well. Chill. Roll out to ¼-inch thickness on floured board and cut into 3-inch squares. To make filling, combine applesauce and walnuts. Add 1 teaspoon of filling to each square. Fold diagonally to form triangle. Crimp edges and sprinkle lightly with sugar. Bake at 375 degrees for about 10 minutes. Melt chocolate chips and butter. Dip half of each triangle in chocolate and let set on waxed paper. YIELD: 2 DOZEN COOKIES.

As a Gift: Present these cookies to the music lover on your list. Include a CD of their favorite Italian opera.

Old-Fashioned Snickerdoodles

½ cup butter or margarine
¾ cup sugar
1 egg
1 teaspoon baking powder
¼ teaspoon salt
1⅔ cups flour
2½ tablespoons sugar mixed with
   1½ teaspoons cinnamon

Combine butter and sugar in large bowl. Add egg and beat until creamy. Add baking powder, salt, and flour. Stir until mixture forms thick dough. Put cinnamon-sugar mixture in small bowl. Shape dough into 1-inch balls. Roll balls in cinnamon-sugar mixture. Place on greased baking sheet. Using bottom of cup, press balls to flatten slightly. Bake at 400 degrees for 10 minutes.

Orange-Iced Cranberry Cookies

½ cup butter, softened
¾ cup sugar
½ cup packed brown sugar
½ cup sour cream
1 teaspoon vanilla
2 eggs
2¼ cups flour

½ teaspoon baking soda
½ teaspoon baking powder
½ teaspoon salt
1 cup chopped fresh cranberries or dried cranberries
1 can orange-flavored buttercream frosting

In large bowl, cream together butter, sugars, sour cream, vanilla, and eggs. Add flour, baking soda, baking powder, and salt. Mix well. Stir in cranberries gently. Drop by teaspoons onto lightly greased baking sheet and bake at 350 degrees for 12 minutes. Cool and frost with frosting. YIELD: 2½ DOZEN COOKIES.

As a Gift: Buy some beautiful navel oranges and arrange them among the cookies in a bread basket you're gifting. Oranges are really good this time of year and always welcome!

Mrs. Santa's Cinnamon Cookies

½ cup butter
½ cup shortening
1 egg yolk
1 tablespoon light corn syrup

2 cups flour
1¼ teaspoons baking soda
1 tablespoon cinnamon

Cream together butter, shortening, egg yolk, and corn syrup. Combine flour, baking soda, and cinnamon. Blend into creamed mixture and chill for 1 hour. Form into balls and place on ungreased baking sheet. Press with fork dipped in sugar. Bake at 375 degrees for 10 to 12 minutes. Cool for 5 minutes before removing from baking sheet. YIELD: 2 DOZEN COOKIES.

As a Gift: Present your cookies on a doily-lined, sturdy plastic plate. Bundle in cellophane and tie with a bow.

Oatmeal Drop Cookies

2 cups flour
1½ cups sugar
1 teaspoon baking powder
½ teaspoon baking soda
½ teaspoon salt
1 teaspoon cinnamon
3 cups old-fashioned rolled oats

1 cup raisins
¾ to 1 cup semisweet chocolate
  chips (optional)
1 cup vegetable oil
2 eggs
½ cup milk

In large bowl, sift together flour, sugar, baking powder, baking soda, salt, and cinnamon. Mix in oats, raisins, and, if desired, chocolate chips. Add oil, eggs, and milk. Mix until thoroughly blended. Drop by teaspoons onto ungreased baking sheet. Bake at 375 degrees for 10 minutes. YIELD: ABOUT 6 DOZEN COOKIES.

Shortbread

1 cup shortening	2 teaspoons vanilla
½ cup sugar	2¾ cups flour
½ cup packed brown sugar	2 teaspoons cream of tartar
3 egg yolks	1 teaspoon baking soda
¼ cup milk	½ teaspoon salt

Cream together shortening, sugars, and egg yolks. Add milk and vanilla. Combine flour, cream of tartar, baking soda, and salt. Stir into creamed mixture. Chill for 1 hour. Roll out to ½-inch thickness on floured board. Cut into long strips and then cut across strips to form 2-inch squares. Place on ungreased baking sheet and bake at 350 degrees for 10 to 12 minutes. YIELD: 3 DOZEN SHORTBREAD SQUARES.

As a Gift: Arrange the shortbread in waxed paper in a square Scottish-looking tin. Include a packet of fine tea or a small tea brewing ball as a gift.

Old-Fashioned Gingersnaps

2 cups dark molasses
½ cup packed brown sugar
½ cup water
1 cup shortening

2 teaspoons ginger
6½ cups flour
2 teaspoons baking soda
½ teaspoon salt

Cook molasses, brown sugar, and water in saucepan on low heat for 15 minutes. Remove from heat and add shortening and ginger. Set aside until cool. Add flour, baking soda, and salt. Mix well. Dough should be very stiff. Chill for 2 hours. Roll out as thin as possible on floured board. Cut into small circles and place on greased baking sheet. Bake at 375 degrees for 6 to 8 minutes or until slightly brown. YIELD: 7 DOZEN COOKIES.

As a Gift: These classic Christmas cookies will present well in a clear cellophane bag with a tent label stapled to the top. Include your greeting on the tent, punch a hole, and tie a ribbon into it.

Plum Jam Cookies

2 sticks (8 ounces) butter
1 cup packed brown sugar
1 egg
¼ cup water
3 cups flour

Pinch salt
1 teaspoon baking powder
1 cup plum (or any other flavor) jam

In large bowl, cream together butter and brown sugar. Beat in egg and water. Sift together flour, salt, and baking powder; stir into creamed mixture until well blended. On lightly floured surface, roll out dough to ¼-inch thickness. Cut with 2-inch round cookie cutter. Place half of cookies on baking sheet and spread ½ teaspoon plum jam in center of each one. With thimble or small cookie cutter, cut center out of remaining cookies. Place these rounds on top of jam-topped cookies to make sandwiches. Press together. Bake at 375 degrees for 10 minutes; remove to wire rack to cool.

Pecan Care Bears

1 cup butter
¼ cup sugar
2 teaspoons vanilla

2 cups flour
½ teaspoon salt
2½ cups chopped pecans

Cream together butter, sugar, and vanilla. Combine flour, salt, and pecans. Mix well. Form into 2-inch balls and place on ungreased baking sheet. Bake at 325 degrees for about 15 minutes. Cool slightly and roll in powdered sugar. YIELD: 3 DOZEN COOKIES.

As a Gift: Arrange these pretty cookies gently in a tall, clear glass jar with a tight-fitting lid. Tie a ribbon at the neck. Use a sticky label attached to the jar to present your greeting.

Gingerbread Men

1 cup packed brown sugar
⅓ cup shortening
1½ cups dark molasses
⅔ cup water
7 cups flour
2 teaspoons baking soda
1 teaspoon salt

2 teaspoons ginger
1 teaspoon allspice
1 teaspoon cloves
1 teaspoon cinnamon
1 (16 ounce) can frosting (any flavor)

Cream together brown sugar and shortening. Add molasses and water. Mix well. Stir in flour, baking soda, salt, and spices. Cover and chill for 2 hours. Roll out one-fourth of dough at a time to ½-inch thickness. Cut with gingerbread man cookie cutter and place cookies on lightly greased baking sheet. Leave plenty of room between each cookie. Bake at 350 degrees for 10 to 12 minutes. Cool, frost, and decorate. YIELD: 3 DOZEN COOKIES.

As a Gift: Wrap each gingerbread man in a clear kitchen bag and tie the top with a ribbon. Give each one a name tag to make him as individual as the child receiving him.

Peppermint Meringue Drops

4 egg whites
¼ teaspoon salt
¼ teaspoon cream of tartar

1 teaspoon peppermint extract
1½ cups sugar

In mixing bowl, beat egg whites, salt, cream of tartar, and extract until soft peaks form. Add sugar gradually until mixture forms stiff peaks. Drop by teaspoons onto parchment-lined baking sheet. Bake at 300 degrees for 20 minutes or until very lightly browned. Let meringue drops harden before removing from baking sheet. YIELD: 1½ DOZEN COOKIES.

As a Gift: Put several meringue drops in a clear plastic bag and tie with ribbon. Place the bag in a small tissue- or cloth-lined basket along with some really good pure chocolate bars. The drops and chocolate are a great combination, so attach a label with that suggestion and your greeting.

Rosemary Crescents

½ cup shortening
1 cup sugar
1 egg
5 cups flour
1 teaspoon baking powder

1 teaspoon baking soda
½ teaspoon salt
1 teaspoon rosemary
1 cup buttermilk

In mixing bowl, cream together shortening, sugar, and egg. In separate bowl, combine flour, baking powder, baking soda, salt, and rosemary. Add to creamed mixture alternately with buttermilk. Chill for 2 hours. Roll out to ½-inch thickness on floured board and cut into circles with cookie cutter. Halve each cookie and gently shape into crescent. Place on greased baking sheet and bake at 350 degrees for 10 minutes. While cookies are still warm, lightly dust with powdered sugar. YIELD: 6 DOZEN CRESCENTS.

As a Gift: Nestle these unusual tea cookies into a gift tin lined with waxed paper. Tie a ribbon around the tin and insert a few sprigs of fresh rosemary into the bow.

Perfect Pumpkin Cookies

2½ cups flour
1 teaspoon baking powder
1 teaspoon baking soda
½ teaspoon salt
2 teaspoons cinnamon
½ teaspoon nutmeg
¼ teaspoon cloves
½ cup butter, softened
1 cup brown sugar

1 (16 ounce) can pumpkin puree
1 egg
1 teaspoon vanilla

ICING:
2 cups powdered sugar
3 tablespoons milk
1 tablespoon butter
1 teaspoon vanilla

In large bowl, combine flour, baking powder, baking soda, salt, and spices. Mix well with whisk; set aside. In separate bowl, cream butter and brown sugar; add pumpkin, egg, and vanilla and beat until creamy. Mix in dry ingredients. Drop on baking sheet by teaspoons and flatten slightly with palm of hand. Bake at 350 degrees for 15 to 20 minutes. To prepare icing, combine powdered sugar, milk, butter, and vanilla. Add more milk as needed for proper consistency.

Allow cookies to cool completely; with fork, drizzle icing over cookies.

Candy

Almond Coconut Clusters

2 cups sugar
½ cup milk
1 tablespoon light corn syrup
1 cup unsweetened flaked coconut

1 cup sliced almonds, toasted
1 teaspoon vanilla
1 teaspoon butter
Dash salt

In heavy saucepan, combine sugar, milk, and corn syrup. Cook to soft ball stage (235 degrees) and remove from heat. Add coconut, almonds, vanilla, butter, and salt. Stir well until mixture starts to thicken. Drop by clusters onto waxed paper, working quickly. Yield: About 2 dozen candies.

As a Gift: Place each cluster into candy or small muffin papers with a holiday design. Line a lidded gift box or tin in a single layer. Slip a handwritten note under the lid.

Butterscotch Delights

1½ cups mini marshmallows
1 cup pecan pieces

2 cups butterscotch chips
½ cup sweetened condensed milk

Butter 9x13-inch pan. Spread marshmallows and pecan pieces evenly on bottom of pan. In saucepan, combine butterscotch chips and condensed milk. Stir constantly over low heat until chips are melted. Pour mixture over marshmallows and nuts in pan. Use spatula to spread mixture evenly. Let stand at room temperature until set. Cut into squares. Store in tightly covered container in refrigerator.

Bull's Eyes

½ cup crunchy peanut butter
6 tablespoons butter, softened
1 tablespoon light corn syrup
1 teaspoon vanilla

2 cups powdered sugar
1 cup graham cracker crumbs
¾ cup semisweet chocolate chips
2 tablespoons shortening

In large bowl, beat peanut butter, butter, corn syrup, and vanilla on medium speed until smooth. Beat in sugar and cracker crumbs on low speed until well mixed. Mixture will look dry. Shape into 1-inch balls. In microwavable bowl, melt chocolate chips and shortening on high for 1 minute. Stir. Microwave for another 30 seconds or until completely melted. With dipping spoon, dip peanut butter balls in chocolate mixture. Place on baking sheet lined with waxed paper. Let chocolate set completely before storing balls in tightly covered container.

Caramel Apples

5 or 6 Granny Smith apples
2 bags wrapped caramels

Wash and dry apples. Remove stems and push popsicle stick deep into stem hole. Unwrap caramels and melt in heavy saucepan over low heat. Stir constantly and do not allow mixture to scorch. When smooth, dip apples within 1 or 2 inches of stick. Let excess drip off and place on waxed paper to cool and set. Dipped apples may be rolled in chopped peanuts, crushed pretzels, or crushed candy canes if desired. YIELD: 5 TO 6 APPLES.

As a Gift: Wrap each apple individually in cellophane and tie with curling ribbon. Present apples one at a time (on coworkers' desks, for example) or together in a lined Christmas basket for a family.

Banana Clusters

1 (12 ounce) package semisweet
    chocolate chips
⅓ cup peanut butter

1 cup unsalted peanuts
1 cup banana chips

Put chocolate chips and peanut butter in large microwavable bowl. Microwave on high for 2 minutes, stirring after 1 minute, or until chips are melted and mixture is smooth. Fold in peanuts and banana chips. Drop by rounded teaspoons onto waxed paper sprayed with butter-flavored nonstick cooking spray. Refrigerate until firm. Store in tightly covered container in refrigerator.

Chocolate-Covered Strawberries

2 cups semisweet chocolate chips
12 large, ripe, long-stemmed strawberries
4 ounces white melting chocolate

Melt chocolate chips according to package instructions. Holding the stem, dip berries into melted chocolate up to the shoulder (some of the bright red of the berry should be visible). Place berries on their sides on waxed paper to set. As dark chocolate firms, melt white chocolate and drizzle in stripes across resting berries. YIELD: 1 DOZEN STRAWBERRIES.

As a Gift: Chocolate-covered strawberries get the blue ribbon for decadent desserts! These treats look so fancy but are so easy to make! Present the berries on a doily-covered dish bundled into cellophane and tied with a festive ribbon.

Caramel Nut Cups

2 cups semisweet chocolate chips
1 tablespoon butter

¾ cup pecan pieces
¾ cup caramel ice-cream topping

In small saucepan over low heat, melt chocolate chips with butter, stirring constantly. Spoon about ½ tablespoon mixture into 36 small foil cups. With back of spoon, spread chocolate up sides of each cup, forming hollow center. Refrigerate until firm. Mix pecan pieces with caramel ice-cream topping. Spoon mixture into chocolate cups. Refrigerate. YIELD: 3 DOZEN CANDIES.

Caramel Popcorn

¼ cup butter
½ cup light corn syrup
1 cup brown sugar
⅔ cup sweetened condensed milk

1 teaspoon vanilla
5 cups popped corn, unpopped
  hulls removed

In large saucepan, combine butter, corn syrup, and brown sugar. Bring to a boil. Add condensed milk and return to a boil, stirring constantly. Remove from heat and stir in vanilla. In large bowl, combine popped corn and caramel mixture, stirring well to coat. With buttered hands, form into balls. Place on waxed paper to cool and set. Wrap balls individually in plastic wrap. YIELD: ABOUT 15 POPCORN BALLS.

Chocolate-Covered Cherries

1 (8 ounce) package milk chocolate melting chocolate
24 large dried sweet cherries

Melt chocolate according to package directions. Using a toothpick, dip each cherry into chocolate until well coated and place on waxed paper. Using another toothpick for leverage, pull dipping pick out of cherry and allow to set. YIELD: 2 DOZEN CHERRIES.

As a Gift: Fill a clear jar with these delectable candies. Be sure it has a tight-fitting lid. Tie a bright red fabric ribbon to the top of the jar. Label the jar with your greeting.

Chocolate-Dipped Dried Apricots

2 dozen whole dried apricots
1 bag white, semisweet, or milk chocolate chips

Melt chocolate chips in deep bowl set in gently simmering water. Do not let water splash into chocolate. When chocolate is completely melted, dip base of each apricot until coated about halfway up. Lay each apricot on waxed paper to harden. YIELD: 2 DOZEN APRICOTS.

As a Gift: Place 2 or 3 apricots into candy papers and tuck them into a box around your gift of a nice pair of gloves or a winter scarf. Cover with a layer of tissue paper.

Cashew Brittle

2 cups milk chocolate chips
¾ cup coarsely chopped cashews
½ cup butter, softened

½ cup sugar
2 tablespoons light corn syrup

Line 9x9-inch pan with foil. Butter foil. Spread chocolate chips evenly over bottom of pan. In saucepan, combine cashews, butter, sugar, and corn syrup. Cook over low heat, stirring constantly until butter is melted and sugar is dissolved. Continue to cook over medium heat until mixture begins to cling together and turns golden brown. Pour mixture over chocolate chips in pan, spreading evenly. Cool. Refrigerate until firm. Remove from pan and break into pieces. Store tightly covered in cool, dry place.

Chocolate-Dipped Candy Canes

1 bag semisweet or milk chocolate chips
20 large candy canes, unwrapped

Melt chocolate chips in deep bowl set in gently simmering water. Do not let water splash into chocolate. When chocolate is completely melted, dip base of each cane until coated about halfway up. Hang canes from their hooks over edge of tall bowl to allow chocolate to harden. YIELD: 20 CANDY CANES.

As a Gift: Present 4 or 5 candy canes in a long cellophane gift bag gathered at the top and tied with ribbon. Or fold the bag top and create your own tent label and staple it on. Make two hole punches in the label and bring a ribbon through it from back to front where it can be tied into a bow. You will have enough to make 4 or 5 gifts.

Chocolate Haystacks

2 cups semisweet chocolate chips
1 (12 ounce) can sweetened condensed milk
2 cups pretzel sticks, broken in ½-inch pieces
1 cup dry roasted peanuts
½ cup mini M&M's

Melt chocolate chips and milk in heavy saucepan over low heat. Stir constantly until melted and smooth. Do not boil. Remove from heat and let rest for 5 minutes. In large bowl, toss pretzel sticks, peanuts, and M&M's until evenly combined. Gently fold in melted chocolate mixture. Working quickly, drop mixture by teaspoons onto baking sheets lined with waxed paper. Chill for at least 2 hours. YIELD: ABOUT 2 DOZEN CANDIES.

As a Gift: Place each candy in a paper wrapper and arrange on a pretty hostess plate you are gifting. Bundle all in cellophane wrap and tie with a bow.

Christmas Mints

1 (8 ounce) package cream cheese, room temperature
¼ to ½ teaspoon flavoring (peppermint, butter, almond, wintergreen, other)
Food coloring
Up to 3 cups powdered sugar
Sugar, as needed

In medium bowl, beat cream cheese, flavoring, and coloring. Gradually add powdered sugar. Mix and knead until mixture reaches consistency of pie dough or putty. Roll into marble-sized balls. Dip in sugar and press firmly into candy mold. Unmold at once onto waxed paper. Once firm, transfer to wire rack and let dry for 2 hours. Store in airtight container. YIELD: ABOUT 6 DOZEN MINTS.

As a Gift: Present these pretty mints in a candy dish you are gifting. Bundle all in cellophane wrap and tie with a velvet bow.

Chocolate Truffles

6 ounces semisweet chocolate
   baking squares
3 tablespoons unsalted butter
2 tablespoons powdered sugar

3 egg yolks
1 tablespoon rum flavoring
½ cup finely grated semisweet
   chocolate

Melt chocolate squares in top of double boiler over boiling water. Blend in butter and powdered sugar and stir until sugar dissolves. Remove from heat and add egg yolks one at a time, beating well after each addition. Stir in rum flavoring. Place mixture in bowl covered with waxed paper overnight, but do not chill. Shape into 1-inch balls and roll in grated chocolate. Set truffles aside for a few days before eating. YIELD: 2 DOZEN TRUFFLES.

Chocolate-Dipped Pretzels

2 dozen pretzel rods or large pretzel twists
1 bag white, semisweet, or milk chocolate chips

Melt chocolate chips in deep bowl set in gently simmering water. Do not let water splash into chocolate. When chocolate is completely melted, dip base of each pretzel until coated about halfway up. Lay each pretzel on waxed paper to harden. YIELD: 2 DOZEN PRETZELS.

As a Gift: Present your gift in clear cellophane gift bags (look for them in cooking and craft stores), sized to fit your pretzels. Bunch the top with ribbon or make a tent label and staple or hot glue it to the top of the bag.

Christmas Crunchies

1 cup butterscotch chips
½ cup crunchy peanut butter
5 cups crisp rice cereal

In saucepan, stir butterscotch chips and peanut butter over low heat until chips are melted. Pour mixture over cereal in large bowl. Stir gently until cereal is completely coated. Drop by teaspoons onto waxed paper. Chill for at least 2 hours.

Divinity Fudge

4 cups sugar
1 cup light corn syrup
½ cup water
¼ teaspoon salt

2 egg whites, beaten until frothy
1 cup chopped nuts (optional)
1 teaspoon vanilla

Boil sugar, corn syrup, water, and salt to soft ball stage (235 degrees). Slowly add hot syrup to egg whites. Beat until mixture looks like fudge; then add nuts and vanilla. Spread into greased 9x13-inch pan. Cool. Cut into cubes.
YIELD: ABOUT 2 DOZEN CUBES.

As a Gift: Wrap fudge cubes in Christmas-colored foil. Present them in a clear jar tied with a pretty ribbon at the neck.

Peanut Brittle

1 cup sugar
½ cup light corn syrup

1 cup salted peanuts
1 teaspoon baking soda

Bring sugar and corn syrup to rolling boil. Stir in peanuts and keep boiling until mixture turns light tan. Remove from heat and add soda. Stir well and pour onto well-buttered jelly roll pan. Cool and break into pieces. YIELD: ABOUT 1 POUND.

As a Gift: Arrange peanut brittle in a candy jar or gift tin lined with waxed paper. Write out an encouraging scripture or one related to Christmas on a small note card. Punch a hole in one end and push a ribbon through. Tie around the top of the jar and make a bow.

Peanut Butter Bark

2 cups milk chocolate chips, divided
2 cups peanut butter chips
1 cup dry roasted peanuts
½ teaspoon salt

Line baking sheet with waxed paper. In large saucepan over low heat, melt 1¾ cups milk chocolate chips, all of the peanut butter chips, and salt, stirring frequently until smooth. Or microwave chips in large bowl for 1 to 2 minutes, stirring every 30 seconds. Stir in remaining ¼ cup chocolate chips until mixture is smooth. Stir in peanuts. Spread mixture on baking sheet lined with waxed paper and chill for 1 hour. Break into pieces and store in tightly covered container. YIELD: ABOUT 2½ DOZEN PIECES.

As a Gift: Present these delicious morsels in a pretty candy bowl you are gifting. Bundle the bowl in brightly decorated Christmas cellophane and tie with a ribbon.

Holiday Chocolate Fudge

3 cups sugar
1½ sticks (12 tablespoons) butter
⅔ cup evaporated milk
1 (12 ounce) package chocolate
  chips

1 (7 ounce) jar marshmallow creme
½ teaspoon salt
½ teaspoon vanilla
1 cup chopped walnuts (optional)

Bring sugar, butter, and milk to full boil, stirring constantly until mixture reaches soft ball stage (235 degrees). Remove from heat and stir in chocolate chips until melted. Add marshmallow creme, salt, vanilla, and nuts. Spread into 9x13-inch pan and cut into cubes when cool. YIELD: 3 POUNDS.

As a Gift: Present fudge cubes wrapped in foil and placed in a sleigh gift holder so the cubes look like wrapped gifts. (These gift containers come in all shapes and sizes at your local craft store.) Attach a bow or bundle it all up in clear cellophane. This recipe is ideal for three or even four gifts.

Crispy Cereal Chocolate Drops

2 cups butterscotch chips
1 cup semisweet chocolate chips
½ cup salted peanuts

4 cups crisp cereal (almost anything will work)

Melt butterscotch chips and chocolate chips over low heat, stirring constantly until smooth. Remove from heat. Add peanuts and cereal. Stir carefully until well coated. Drop by teaspoons onto waxed paper. Chill until firm. YIELD: 8 DOZEN DROPS.

Peanut Butter Kisses

1 cup dark corn syrup
1 cup peanut butter
1½ cups nonfat dry milk

1 cup powdered sugar
3 cups crisp rice cereal

Mix corn syrup and peanut butter together well. Add dry milk and powdered sugar. Stir until mixture is smooth. Add cereal. Roll into marble-sized balls. Let set on waxed paper until firm. YIELD: 2 DOZEN KISSES.

As a Gift: Twist each ball into pretty candy wrappers and scatter them in a gift basket with a new set of Christmas kitchen towels.

Delicious Date Balls

16 ounces dates, pitted and chopped
2 cups sugar
2 eggs, beaten
½ cup butter
¼ teaspoon salt
1 teaspoon vanilla
3½ cups crisp rice cereal
1 cup chopped nuts
Sweetened flaked coconut

Combine dates, sugar, eggs, butter, and salt. Cook over low heat until smooth. Don't boil. Remove from heat and add vanilla. In large bowl, mix cereal and nuts. Pour hot mixture over cereal mixture and stir well. With buttered hands, form mixture into balls. Roll in coconut. YIELD: 4 DOZEN BALLS.

As a Gift: Present these pretty candies on a pedestal plate lined with a doily. Stretch plastic wrap over the candy and top with a bow.

Rock Candy

2 cups sugar
½ cup light corn syrup
½ cup water

½ teaspoon flavored oil
Food coloring
1 cup powdered sugar

Using candy thermometer, cook sugar, corn syrup, and water to hard crack stage (300 degrees). Remove from heat and add oil and food coloring. Pour quickly onto greased jelly roll pan. Cool and then press a hard object into candy to fracture it into small pieces. Place cool candy in bag with powdered sugar. Shake to coat lightly. Place candy in colander and shake again to remove all but light dusting of sugar. YIELD: ABOUT 1½ POUNDS.

As a Gift: This candy gives the appearance of stained glass and presents beautifully in a clear glass candy dish you are gifting. Tip: Make several batches, each with a different flavoring and color. Mix the colors for presentation.

Toffee

1 cup pecan halves
1½ cups brown sugar

1 cup butter
1 teaspoon vanilla

Spread pecan pieces on buttered jelly roll pan. Set aside. In saucepan, boil brown sugar and butter until candy thermometer reads 290 degrees. Remove from heat and stir in vanilla. Pour over pecan pieces. Let cool completely. Break into pieces.

Turtles

1 cup pecan halves
36 caramels, unwrapped
½ cup milk chocolate chips, melted

Preheat oven to 325 degrees. Arrange pecan halves flat side down in clusters of 4 on greased baking sheet. Place 1 caramel in middle of each cluster. Heat in oven until caramels soften, about 4 to 8 minutes. Remove from oven. Flatten caramels slightly. Cool briefly; then remove from pan to waxed paper. Swirl melted chocolate on top of each cluster.

Pecan Pralines

3 cups sugar
1 cup milk
2 tablespoons light corn syrup
1 teaspoon vanilla

1 tablespoon butter
½ teaspoon salt
3 cups pecan halves

In large saucepan, cook sugar, milk, and corn syrup to soft ball stage (235 degrees). Add vanilla, butter, salt, and pecans. Remove from heat and stir until mixture begins to thicken and turn slightly opaque. Quickly drop by teaspoons onto waxed paper. Work fast, as pralines set up quickly! YIELD: 25 TO 30 PRALINES.

As a Gift: Line a gift tin with waxed paper and stack the pralines with waxed paper between layers. Pack the candy snugly so it doesn't shift around and break.

Festive

BREADS

❧

Unless we make Christmas an occasion to share
our blessings, all the snow in Alaska won't make it white.
BING CROSBY

You, Jesus, are the Bread of Life—holy sustenance for starving souls. You alone fill the hungry with good things. Make us conscious, Father, of all those around us who crave Living Bread! Amen.

"I am the living bread that came down from heaven. Whoever eats this bread will live forever."

JOHN 6:51 NIV

Butter Pecan Bread

2¼ cups flour
2 teaspoons baking powder
½ teaspoon baking soda
½ teaspoon salt
¼ teaspoon cinnamon
¼ teaspoon nutmeg

1 cup brown sugar
1 egg, beaten
1 cup buttermilk
2 tablespoons butter, melted
1 cup chopped pecans

Sift flour, baking powder, baking soda, salt, and spices into bowl. Stir in brown sugar. Set aside. In separate bowl, combine egg, buttermilk, and butter. Add to flour mixture and blend well. Stir in chopped pecans. Turn batter into greased and floured 5x9-inch loaf pan. Bake at 350 degrees for 45 to 50 minutes or until wooden pick inserted in center comes out clean. YIELD: 1 LOAF.

Date Bread

¼ cup shortening
¾ cup boiling water
1 cup chopped dates
¾ cup chopped nuts
½ teaspoon salt

1½ teaspoons baking soda
2 eggs
1 cup sugar
1½ cups flour
½ teaspoon vanilla

Melt shortening in boiling water and pour over dates, nuts, salt, and baking soda. Let stand for 15 minutes. Add eggs, sugar, flour, and vanilla. Mix well. Pour into lightly greased and floured loaf pan. Bake at 350 degrees for 1 hour. YIELD: 1 LARGE LOAF.

As a Gift: Wrap bread first in waxed paper and then in foil. With raffia or other Christmas ribbon, tie a bow around the loaf. Line a bread basket with a set of red or green cloth napkins and place the bread inside.

Em's Rusks

4 cups self-rising flour
1 cup sweetened flaked coconut
2 cups wheat bran
1 cup salted sunflower seeds
¼ cup sunflower oil

3 teaspoons baking powder
1 teaspoon salt
4 cups buttermilk
1 pound (4 sticks) margarine
1 cup honey

In large bowl, mix all ingredients together. Spoon batter into two greased and floured loaf pans. Bake at 350 degrees for 1 hour. When cool, cut bread into slices and place on baking sheets. Slice each slab into 4 pieces, like fingerlings. Let bread dry out overnight (about 12 hours) in 200-degree oven. YIELD: ABOUT 100 CRUNCHY PIECES.

As a Gift: This classic South African tea bread is very healthy and just sweet enough to complement any hot drink. Place dried fingerlings like dominoes in a quality lidded Christmas tin that you will gift. Line it with waxed paper at the bottom and between each layer. Include a label: *Rusks: delicious South African tea crisps.*

Christmas Sweet Bread

1 cup butter
1 cup sugar
1 cup sorghum syrup
3 teaspoons baking powder

⅛ teaspoon baking soda
¼ teaspoon salt
3 cups flour
4 eggs, beaten

Over medium heat, melt butter in saucepan. Add sugar and syrup. Heat until lukewarm. In mixing bowl, combine baking powder, baking soda, and salt with flour. Add to first mixture. Add well-beaten eggs and mix thoroughly. Pour into greased loaf pan and bake at 275 degrees for 18 to 20 minutes or until done. YIELD: 1 LOAF.

Banana Bread

½ cup butter
1 cup sugar
2 eggs
2 cups flour
1 teaspoon baking soda

½ teaspoon salt
3 very ripe (black) bananas
½ cup whole milk
1 teaspoon vanilla

Cream together butter, sugar, and eggs. Mix together flour, baking soda, and salt. Add to creamed mixture. Add bananas, milk, and vanilla. Blend well and pour into greased loaf pan. Bake at 350 degrees for about 1 hour. YIELD: 1 LOAF.

As a Gift: Wrap the bread first in waxed paper and then in foil. A bow or ribbon tied around it is sufficient. You may want to place the bread in a basket along with a pretty set of small paper Christmas napkins—entertainers go through a lot of these at the holidays! Garnish with a small bunch of bananas if your basket is roomy enough.

Cheese Biscuits

2 cups sifted flour
3 teaspoons baking powder
½ teaspoon salt
¼ cup shortening
½ cup shredded swiss or
   cheddar cheese

⅔ cup milk
1 egg, lightly beaten
2 to 3 tablespoons butter, melted

Sift dry ingredients together. Cut in shortening and cheese, mixing well. Add milk and egg, stirring quickly until soft dough is formed. Turn onto lightly floured surface and knead into smooth ball. Roll lightly to 2-inch thickness and cut into rounds with floured biscuit cutter. Place on ungreased baking sheet and bake at 375 degrees for 12 to 15 minutes. Brush with melted butter immediately after removing from oven.

Christmas Morning Cinnamon Rolls

1 loaf frozen bread dough
1 stick (8 tablespoons) butter, melted
1 cup packed brown sugar

2 teaspoons cinnamon
½ cup chopped walnuts
½ cup sweetened dried cranberries

Allow frozen dough to thaw but not rise. Roll out into thin rectangle. Spread with butter and top with sugar, cinnamon, walnuts, and cranberries. Roll tightly, beginning with long edge. Pinch along seam to seal. Cut into 12 slices and place in lightly greased oblong baking pan. Let rise covered with waxed paper for about 1 hour. Bake at 350 degrees for about 20 minutes. Don't overbake. Upon removing from oven, immediately invert onto waxed paper to cool. YIELD: 1 DOZEN ROLLS.

As a Gift: Plan to bake these rolls the same day you are giving them. Wrap the whole oblong of connected rolls first in waxed paper and then in foil. Present your gift in a pretty basket lined with a tea towel. If you like, include a container of whipped butter.

Christmas Pound Cake

1 pound butter
2 cups sugar
4 cups flour
12 eggs
2 teaspoons vanilla

1½ teaspoons lemon extract
½ teaspoon salt
½ teaspoon nutmeg
1 cup sour cream

In large bowl, cream butter and sugar. Gradually add flour and eggs. Add remaining ingredients and mix well. Turn into greased loaf pans and bake at 325 degrees for 1 hour. Increase temperature to 350 degrees and bake for another 15 minutes. Cool completely. Wrap in foil and tie with a festive ribbon.

Sweet Potato Biscuits

4 cups flour
⅔ cup sugar
2 tablespoons baking powder
1½ teaspoons salt

2 cups sweet potatoes, cooked,
  mashed, and warm
½ cup vegetable oil or shortening
¼ cup milk

In large bowl, mix all ingredients together. Separate dough into pieces and roll into average-size biscuits. Place on greased baking sheet and bake at 475 degrees for 15 minutes. YIELD: 36 BISCUITS.

Parmesan Breadsticks

1 (1 pound) loaf french bread
¾ cup butter or margarine, melted
¼ cup grated parmesan cheese

Cut bread loaf into 5 pieces, each about 4 inches long. Cut each piece lengthwise into 6 sticks. Brush sides with melted butter and sprinkle with parmesan cheese. Place on ungreased jelly roll pan. Bake at 425 degrees for about 8 minutes or until golden. YIELD: ABOUT 30 BREADSTICKS.

Easy Cinnamon Rolls

1 loaf frozen bread dough
½ cup soft butter
¾ cup brown sugar

½ cup chopped nuts
½ teaspoon salt
Cinnamon

Thaw bread dough in plastic bag just until pliable. Roll out to ¼-inch thickness. Spread with butter. Sprinkle with brown sugar, chopped nuts, salt, and cinnamon. Roll up tightly, starting with long side, and pinch edges to seal. Cut into 12 equal rounds and place in greased baking pan. Cover and let rise for about 1 hour. Bake at 350 degrees for 20 minutes. To prevent rolls from sticking to pan, invert onto waxed paper immediately. Yield: 1 dozen rolls.

Gingerbread

2¼ cups flour
⅓ cup sugar
1 cup dark molasses
¾ cup hot water
½ cup shortening
1 egg

1 teaspoon baking soda
¾ teaspoon salt
1¼ teaspoons cinnamon
1 teaspoon ginger
Whipped topping

Combine all ingredients except whipped topping in large bowl. Pour into greased 9x9-inch pan. Bake at 325 degrees for 50 minutes. Cut into squares and serve warm with whipped topping.

Granny's Corn Bread

2 tablespoons shortening
2 tablespoons butter
1 cup self-rising cornmeal
¾ cup self-rising flour

½ cup sugar
1 cup milk
1 egg
2 tablespoons vegetable oil

Measure shortening and butter into cool iron skillet. Place in oven at 425 degrees. Mix remaining ingredients in order listed. Pour into hot skillet from oven. Bake for 20 to 30 minutes until golden brown.

Holiday Muffins

½ cup vegetable oil
3 eggs
¼ cup brown sugar
2 teaspoons vanilla
1 carrot, peeled and grated
1 apple, peeled and grated
½ cup golden raisins
½ cup sweetened flaked coconut
1 cup flour

½ cup old-fashioned rolled oats
¼ cup wheat germ
½ cup chopped walnuts
1 teaspoon baking soda
1 teaspoon ginger
½ teaspoon baking powder
¼ teaspoon salt
Dash nutmeg

In mixing bowl, beat together oil, eggs, brown sugar, and vanilla until well blended. Add remaining ingredients. Mix on medium speed just until blended. Do not overmix. Divide batter into greased muffin tins, filling to top of each cup. Bake at 375 degrees for about 20 minutes.

Hominy Bread

1 cup boiled hominy
1½ cups milk
¾ cup molasses
1 cup cornmeal
1 cup flour

1 tablespoon baking soda
1 teaspoon baking powder
1 teaspoon salt
1 egg, beaten
1 tablespoon shortening, melted

In large bowl, mash hominy. Add milk and molasses to mashed hominy and beat together. In separate bowl, combine cornmeal, flour, baking soda, baking powder, and salt. Slowly add dry mixture to hominy mixture. Add beaten egg and melted shortening. Turn into greased loaf pan. Bake at 350 degrees for about 35 minutes. YIELD: 1 LOAF.

Honey Apple Raisin Nut Bread

1 cup honey
½ cup shortening
2 eggs, beaten
2 cups flour
1 teaspoon baking soda
¼ teaspoon salt
½ teaspoon cinnamon

⅛ teaspoon allspice
⅛ teaspoon cloves
1 cup applesauce
1 cup quick-cooking oats
1 cup chopped nuts
1 cup raisins

In large bowl, blend honey and shortening. Mix in beaten eggs and beat until fluffy and light. In separate bowl, sift together flour, salt, baking soda, cinnamon, allspice, and cloves. Add dry mixture to honey mixture a little at a time, alternating with applesauce. Stir in oats, nuts, and raisins. Pour into greased loaf pan and bake at 325 degrees for 1 hour. YIELD: 1 LOAF.

Apple Bread

2 medium apples, peeled and coarsely grated
2 tablespoons lemon juice
3 cups flour
1½ teaspoons baking soda
1 teaspoon salt
2½ teaspoons pumpkin pie spice

¾ cup shortening
1¼ cups packed brown sugar
3 eggs, room temperature
1½ teaspoons vanilla
¾ cup strong tea, room temperature
½ cup chopped nuts

In small bowl, mix grated apples with lemon juice and set aside. In separate bowl, combine flour, baking soda, salt, and spice; mix thoroughly and set aside. In another bowl, cream shortening and brown sugar. Add eggs one at a time, beating well after each addition. Stir in apples and vanilla. Stir in flour mixture a little at a time, alternating with tea. Stir in nuts with last addition of dry ingredients. Pour into two greased 4x8-inch loaf pans. Bake at 350 degrees for 1 hour or until bread tests done. Let stand for 5 minutes; remove from pans and cool on wire rack. YIELD: 2 LOAVES.

Pumpkin Muffins

2½ cups pumpkin puree
4 eggs
1 cup vegetable oil
1 cup water
4 cups flour
2¾ cups sugar
1¾ teaspoons baking soda

½ teaspoon baking powder
1 tablespoon cinnamon
1 tablespoon nutmeg
1 tablespoon cloves
1 teaspoon salt
1¼ cups raisins
¾ cup chopped walnuts

In large bowl, mix pumpkin, eggs, oil, and water. In another bowl, sift flour, sugar, baking soda, baking powder, cinnamon, nutmeg, cloves, and salt. Stir into pumpkin mixture. Add raisins and nuts. Line muffin tin cups with paper liners and fill each almost to top. Bake at 375 degrees for 15 minutes. YIELD: 3½ DOZEN MUFFINS.

Honey Wheat Bread

1½ cups water
1 cup cream-style cottage cheese
½ cup honey
¼ cup butter
6 cups flour, divided
1 egg

1 cup whole-wheat flour
2 tablespoons sugar
2 teaspoons salt
2 packages active dry yeast
Shortening
Extra butter

Heat water, cottage cheese, honey, and butter in medium saucepan over medium heat until very warm but not boiling. In large bowl, combine 2 cups flour with warm mixture. Add egg, whole-wheat flour, sugar, salt, and yeast. Beat for 2 minutes. By hand, stir in remaining 4 cups flour to make stiff dough. Knead on well-floured surface until smooth and elastic (about 2 minutes). Place in greased bowl. Cover and let rise in warm place until light and doubled in size (45 to 60 minutes). Grease two loaf pans with shortening. Punch down dough; divide and shape into two loaves. Place in greased pans. Cover; let loaves rise in warm place until doubled in size. Bake at 350 degrees for 40 to 50 minutes until loaves are deep golden brown and sound hollow when tapped. Immediately remove from pans. Brush with butter. YIELD: 2 LOAVES.

Monkey Bread

3 large tubes refrigerated biscuits, separated
1 teaspoon cinnamon

½ cup sugar
½ cup margarine, melted
¾ cup firmly packed brown sugar

Cut each biscuit into quarters. Combine cinnamon and sugar; roll biscuit pieces in mixture, coating each piece well. Place in greased Bundt pan. Mix margarine and brown sugar; pour over biscuits. Bake at 350 degrees for 20 to 30 minutes.

Mayonnaise Biscuits

1 cup whole milk
1 tablespoon sugar

2 tablespoons mayonnaise
2 cups self-rising flour

In large bowl, mix all ingredients. Spoon into greased muffin tins. Bake at 375 degrees for 15 minutes or until golden brown.

Christmas Morning Blueberry Biscuits

2¼ cups flour, divided
½ cup sugar
1 tablespoon baking powder
½ teaspoon grated lemon peel
¾ teaspoon salt
¼ teaspoon baking soda
⅓ cup shortening
1 egg, lightly beaten
¾ cup buttermilk

¾ cup frozen blueberries, do not thaw

TOPPING:
3 tablespoons butter, melted
2 tablespoons sugar
¼ teaspoon cinnamon
Dash nutmeg

In large bowl, mix 2 cups flour with sugar, baking powder, lemon peel, salt, and baking soda. Cut in shortening until mixture is crumbly. In separate bowl, combine egg and buttermilk. Stir into flour mixture. Stir in frozen blueberries. Sprinkle remaining ¼ cup flour on flat surface. Flour fingers and gently knead dough just until it begins to hold together. Pat dough into ½-inch-thick rectangle. Cut with floured 2-inch round cutter. Place biscuits 2 inches apart on lightly greased baking sheet. Bake in center of preheated 400-degree oven for 12 to 15 minutes or until lightly browned. In mixing bowl, combine all topping ingredients and brush over warm biscuits.

Cinnamon Swirl Bread

1 loaf frozen bread dough
1 stick (8 tablespoons) butter,
 softened
1 cup packed brown sugar

2 teaspoons cinnamon
¼ teaspoon salt
½ cup chopped nuts
¼ cup raisins

Allow frozen dough to thaw but not rise. Roll out into short rectangle; this bread will be baked in a loaf pan, so size is important when rolling out dough. Spread butter over all. Mix brown sugar, cinnamon, and salt. Sprinkle over butter. Top with nuts and raisins. Tightly roll dough from one short end to other. Place in large greased loaf pan and let rise, about 1 hour. Bake at 350 degrees for about 30 minutes. YIELD: 1 LARGE LOAF.

As a Gift: When bread is cool, wrap first in waxed paper and then in foil. Place the bread in a lined box and surround it with an assortment of jarred baking spices: cinnamon, nutmeg, cloves, ginger, cinnamon sticks, whatever you like!

Cranberry Bread

2 cups flour
½ teaspoon salt
1½ teaspoons baking powder
1 cup sugar
2 teaspoons baking soda
2 tablespoons hot water

1 egg, beaten
1 tablespoon butter, melted
½ cup orange juice
1 cup cooked cranberries (canned are fine)
1 cup chopped nuts

Combine flour, salt, baking powder, and sugar, leaving well in center. Dissolve baking soda in hot water and add along with egg, butter, and orange juice. Blend well. Add cranberries and nuts. Pour into two lightly greased and floured loaf pans. Bake at 350 degrees for 1 hour. YIELD: 2 LOAVES.

As a Gift: Wrap cooled loaves first in waxed paper and then in foil. Put a Christmas bow on each. Present your gift on a serving tray you are gifting. Line the tray with a pretty Christmas runner and include a new bread knife.

Oatmeal Muffins

1 cup flour
¼ cup sugar
3 teaspoons baking powder
½ teaspoon salt

¼ cup shortening
1 cup quick-cooking oats
1 cup milk
1 egg, beaten

Combine flour, sugar, baking powder, and salt. Cut in shortening until mixture is crumbly. Add oats and mix well. Gently stir in milk and egg. Spoon into greased muffin tin and bake at 400 degrees for 15 minutes. Cool in tin and remove gently. YIELD: 1 DOZEN MUFFINS.

Nana's Banana Bread

1 cup sugar
⅓ cup butter or vegetable shortening
2 eggs, beaten
3 small overripe bananas, mashed
2½ cups flour, divided

1 teaspoon baking soda
6 tablespoons buttermilk
1 teaspoon vanilla
1 teaspoon lemon juice
Pinch salt
Chopped nuts (optional)

In mixing bowl, cream together sugar and butter. Add eggs and bananas. Add 1 cup flour. In separate bowl, stir baking soda into buttermilk and add to mixture. Add remaining 1½ cups flour, vanilla, lemon juice, and salt. Add chopped nuts if desired. Pour into greased and floured loaf pan. Bake at 350 degrees for 45 minutes to 1 hour, testing with toothpick for doneness. Cool for about 5 minutes and remove from pan to wire rack. YIELD: 1 LOAF.

Pumpkin Corn Bread

1½ cups cornmeal
½ cup whole-wheat flour
1 tablespoon baking powder
3 tablespoons sugar
1 teaspoon cinnamon

1 teaspoon salt
1 egg, beaten
3 tablespoons vegetable oil
¾ cup pumpkin puree
1½ cups milk

In large bowl, sift dry ingredients. In separate bowl, blend egg, oil, pumpkin, and milk. Combine with dry mixture and mix lightly. Pour into greased 8x8-inch pan. Bake at 350 degrees for 30 to 35 minutes.

South African Overnight Bread

2 cakes compressed yeast or 2 packages dry yeast
2½ quarts water
3 cups sugar
2 cups butter or margarine

1 (14 ounce) can sweetened condensed milk
2 teaspoons salt
10 cups flour
4 eggs, well beaten

In saucepan, slowly heat yeast, water, sugar, butter, and condensed milk. In large bowl, combine salt and flour; add eggs and warm milk mixture to flour and knead well. Cover and let rise in warm place overnight. Form into balls and place on baking sheets. Cover and let rise again. Bake at 375 degrees for 45 minutes.

Pumpkin Bread

1½ cups sugar
2 eggs
½ cup vegetable oil
1 cup pumpkin puree
¼ cup water

1½ cups flour
1 teaspoon baking soda
½ teaspoon baking powder
½ teaspoon salt
½ teaspoon pumpkin pie spice

Cream together sugar, eggs, oil, pumpkin, and water. Set aside. Mix together flour, baking soda, baking powder, salt, and spice. Combine with creamed mixture and mix well. Spoon into lightly greased and floured loaf pan and bake at 350 degrees for about 1 hour. YIELD: 1 LOAF.

As a Gift: Wrap the bread first in waxed paper and then in foil. Present your gift in an open, lined Christmas basket and include a pretty tablecloth or Christmas table runner. Tie an outrageously big bow on the basket handle!

Zucchini Bread

1 cup vegetable oil
3 eggs
1 teaspoon vanilla
2 cups flour
2 cups sugar
1 tablespoon cinnamon
2 teaspoons baking soda

¼ teaspoon baking powder
1 teaspoon salt
2 cups unpeeled zucchini, coarsely
  grated and packed down
½ cup raisins
½ cup chopped walnuts

Combine oil, eggs, and vanilla; set aside. Combine flour, sugar, cinnamon, baking soda, baking powder, and salt. Add to wet ingredients and mix well. Fold in zucchini, raisins, and nuts. Mix well. Pour into two greased and floured loaf pans and bake at 350 degrees for 1 hour. YIELD: 2 LOAVES.

As a Gift: Wrap each loaf of cooled bread first in waxed paper and then in foil. Tie a velvet ribbon around each and arrange in a green tissue–lined box among a pretty set of Christmas tree ornaments.

Merrymaking:
PARTY DISHES
to Feed a Crowd

Christmas means fellowship,
feasting, giving and receiving,
a time of good cheer, home.
W. J. TUCKER

Lord, our souls are hungry for You. Feed us on Your wonderful Word and help us sense Your presence in all the circumstances of life. Grow us through joy as well as adversity to realize You are ever in control, always with us. Amen.

The LORD of Heaven's Armies will spread a wonderful feast for all the people of the world. It will be a delicious banquet with clear, well-aged wine and choice meat.

ISAIAH 25:6 NLT

Apple-Orange Punch

1 (6 ounce) can frozen orange juice concentrate, thawed

1 (6 ounce) can frozen lemonade concentrate, thawed

1 quart apple juice, chilled

2 quarts ginger ale, chilled

1 pint orange sherbet

Mix concentrates and apple juice in large punch bowl. Just before serving, stir in ginger ale and spoon sherbet into bowl.

Broccoli Squares

2 (8 ounce) tubes refrigerated crescent rolls, unseparated

2 (8 ounce) packages cream cheese, softened

1 cup mayonnaise

1 (1 ounce) package ranch dressing mix

1 head broccoli, chopped into small pieces

3 roma (plum) tomatoes, chopped

1 cup shredded cheddar cheese

Arrange crescent roll dough in 4 rectangles on lightly greased baking sheet. Bake at 375 degrees for 12 minutes or until golden brown. Cool completely. In medium bowl, mix cream cheese, mayonnaise, and dry ranch dressing mix. Spread evenly over baked crust. Sprinkle with broccoli and tomatoes. Top with cheddar cheese and serve.

Christmas Coffee Punch

3 quarts water

½ cup instant coffee granules

2 cups sugar

1 (8 ounce) can chocolate syrup

3 quarts milk

3 quarts vanilla ice cream

In large saucepan mix water and coffee and bring to a boil. Add sugar and chocolate syrup. Chill overnight. Add milk and ice cream 30 minutes before serving. YIELD: 24 TO 36 SERVINGS.

Corn and Bacon Dip

1 (8 ounce) package cream cheese, softened
1¼ cups sour cream
1 teaspoon minced garlic
1 teaspoon hot sauce
1 cup white shoepeg corn
½ teaspoon salt
½ pound bacon, fried crisp and crumbled
1 bag corn or tortilla chips

Combine all ingredients except bacon and chips; chill. When ready to serve, sprinkle crumbled bacon on top. Serve with warm corn or tortilla chips. YIELD: 3 CUPS.

Cranberry Pecan Spread

2 cups cream-style cottage cheese
2 tablespoons sour cream
1 tablespoon brown sugar
½ cup chopped pecans, toasted
½ cup dried cranberries
1 teaspoon grated lemon peel
1 loaf french bread

Combine first 6 ingredients and mix well. Chill and serve on crusty french bread slices. YIELD: 2 CUPS.

Cream Cheese Pinwheels

2 (8 ounce) packages cream cheese, softened
1 (4 ounce) can diced green chilies
1 (4 ounce) can chopped black olives
1 (2 ounce) jar diced pimentos
3 to 4 flour tortillas

Mix first 4 ingredients together and spread on tortillas. Roll up gently and slice. Serve chilled. YIELD: ABOUT 2 DOZEN PINWHEELS.

Bacon-Wrapped Water Chestnuts

1 pound bacon
2 cans whole water chestnuts
Teriyaki glaze

Cut bacon slices in half and fry until almost done but still limp enough to wrap around water chestnuts. Secure bacon to chestnut with toothpick. Dip each into bowl of teriyaki glaze and place on foil-lined baking sheet. Bake at 400 degrees until dark and crispy. Watch carefully so they don't burn. YIELD: 30 CHESTNUTS.

Christmas Tradition Gyozas

1 tube high-quality breakfast sausage

1 package chopped cabbage (about 3 cups)

2 green onions, snipped

1 teaspoon Worcestershire sauce

1 teaspoon each ginger, chopped garlic, salt, and pepper

1 package square wonton wrappers

Soy sauce and picante sauce

Mix sausage, veggies, Worcestershire, and seasonings. Lay out several wonton wrappers at a time. With your finger, slightly dampen edges with water. Place small amount of meat mixture in center of each wrapper. Fold over to form triangles and pinch moistened edges together to close. Deep fry in hot oil for about 1 minute (5 to 6 gyozas should be float frying at one time); flip and fry other side for another minute. Gyozas should be deep golden brown. Drain each batch well on paper towels. Eat hot, dipped in equal parts soy sauce and picante sauce. YIELD: 50 GYOZAS.

Dressed Eggs

6 to 7 hard-boiled eggs
¼ cup mayonnaise, more or less depending on desired consistency
½ teaspoon spicy mustard
1 tablespoon dried minced onion
¼ teaspoon garlic salt
¼ teaspoon seasoned or regular salt
¼ teaspoon celery salt
¼ teaspoon pepper
¼ teaspoon paprika
12 to 14 sliced olives or pimento pieces for garnish

Carefully peel cooled eggs and slice lengthwise. Pop out yolks into small bowl and arrange whites on plate. Mash yolks together with remaining ingredients until well blended. Pipe or spoon into whites. Garnish each with sliced olives or pimento pieces. YIELD: 12 TO 14 HALVES.

Double Lime Punch

2 cups lime sherbet, softened
1 (6 ounce) can frozen limeade concentrate, thawed
2 cups cold water
1 (2 liter) bottle ginger ale

Mix first 3 ingredients together in punch bowl. Add ginger ale last and stir gently. YIELD: 12 CUPS.

Fruit Dip

1 (8 ounce) package cream cheese, softened

¾ cup dark brown sugar

¼ cup white sugar

2 teaspoons vanilla

Dash salt

Combine all ingredients and chill well. Serve with whole stemmed strawberries, apple or pear slices, or any other fruit hefty enough to dip. YIELD: 1½ CUPS.

Golden Christmas Punch

1 (6 ounce) can frozen orange juice concentrate, thawed

1 (6 ounce) can frozen lemonade concentrate, thawed

16 ounces water

1 (12 ounce) can apricot nectar

2 cups pineapple juice

½ cup lemon juice

32 ounces ginger ale, chilled

Combine orange and lemonade concentrate with water. Add nectar, pineapple juice, and lemon juice; blend well. Chill. Just before serving, add cold ginger ale. YIELD: 15 CUPS.

Cocktail Meatballs

1½ cups chili sauce
1 cup grape jelly
2 teaspoons mustard
1 pound ground beef

½ teaspoon salt
1 egg, beaten
3 tablespoons fine bread crumbs

Combine chili sauce, jelly, and mustard and pour into slow cooker. Cover and cook on high while making meatballs. Work salt, egg, and bread crumbs into meat until well blended. Shape into bite-size meatballs. Place on baking sheet and bake at 400 degrees for 15 minutes. Drain fat and add to slow cooker. Stir gently to cover. Cook on low for 6 hours. Serve skewered on toothpicks.

YIELD: 2 DOZEN MEATBALLS.

Four-Cheese Ball

1 small jar pimento cheese spread

1 small jar Old English spread

½ cup crumbled blue cheese

1 (8 ounce) package cream cheese, softened

1 dozen green olives, chopped

2 teaspoons dried minced onion

¼ teaspoon cayenne pepper

1 dash each Worcestershire sauce and liquid smoke

Salt and pepper to taste

¼ cup chopped pecans

Variety of crackers

Bring first 4 ingredients to room temperature. Combine all ingredients except pecans and crackers. Mix well and refrigerate. When cool, shape into ball and roll in pecans. Serve with a variety of crackers. Yield: 1 large cheese ball.

Jalapeño Dill Dip

1 small jar dill pickles
1 jalapeño pepper, seeded (canned or fresh)
⅔ cup sugar

½ teaspoon salt
1 (4 ounce) block cream cheese
Variety of crackers

Mix first 4 ingredients in blender until fairly smooth. Pour over cream cheese and serve with crackers. Very spicy! YIELD: 8 TO 10 SERVINGS.

Milk Punch

1 quart cold milk
1 (46 ounce) can or bottle apricot juice
1 (6 ounce) can frozen pink lemonade concentrate, thawed

1 quart vanilla ice cream, softened
1 quart orange sherbet
1 quart ginger ale

Mix first 5 ingredients together in punch bowl. Add ginger ale last and stir gently. YIELD: 16 CUPS.

Olive Crescents

1 tube refrigerated crescent rolls
½ cup grated Italian cheese (romano, parmesan, etc.)
2 dozen green olives

Separate crescent roll dough along perforated triangles. Gently flatten each triangle with rolling pin and cut each into 3 triangles. Sprinkle cheese on each triangle and place an olive in the center. Roll up and bake at 350 degrees for about 8 minutes. Serve immediately. YIELD: 24 CRESCENTS.

Party Punch Ring

1 small package lemon gelatin
1 cup hot water
2 cups cold water
2 cups sugar
1 (46 ounce) can pineapple juice
1 (6 ounce) can frozen orange juice
  concentrate, thawed
2 liters ginger ale

Dissolve gelatin in 1 cup hot water. When completely dissolved, add remaining ingredients (except ginger ale) and mix well. Freeze in Bundt pan or ring mold of your choice. Remove from freezer to begin thawing 1 hour before serving. Unmold into empty punch bowl and add ginger ale. Ring will continue to thaw, releasing flavor into the ginger ale as it melts. Keep adding ginger ale as punch gets low. YIELD: 12 TO 15 SERVINGS.

Pita Poppers

1 cup mayonnaise
1 small onion, finely chopped
½ cup slivered almonds
1½ cups finely shredded
  cheddar cheese
½ pound bacon, fried crisp
  and crumbled
1 package pita bread, halved
  and cut into triangles
  (or use mini pita bites)

Combine first 5 ingredients. Spread on pita triangles and bake at 400 degrees for 8 to 10 minutes. YIELD: 8 SERVINGS. (Increase ingredients according to number of guests.)

Party Pecans

1 egg white
1 teaspoon water
1 pound pecan halves

1 cup sugar
1 teaspoon cinnamon
1 teaspoon salt

In large bowl, whip egg white and water to froth. Add pecans and coat well. In separate bowl, combine sugar, cinnamon, and salt. Add to pecans, using fingers to make sure all are coated. Shake off excess sugar mixture and spread on foil-lined baking sheet. Bake at 225 degrees for 60 to 90 minutes, stirring every 15 minutes. Pecans will crisp up as they cool. YIELD: 2 CUPS.

Holiday Salsa

1 (28 ounce) can diced tomatoes
1 (2 ounce) can chopped black olives
1 (2 ounce) can diced green chilies
3 green onions, chopped
3 tablespoons olive oil

2 teaspoons hot sauce
1½ tablespoons red wine vinegar
½ teaspoon garlic salt
½ teaspoon pepper
Tortilla chips

Combine all ingredients except chips in large bowl and mix well. Cover and chill for several hours before serving with warm tortilla chips. YIELD: 3 CUPS.

Party Nibbles

2 cups toasted oats cereal

2 cups toasted corn squares cereal

2 cups pretzel sticks

1 cup shoestring potatoes

1 pound salted mixed nuts

3 tablespoons Worcestershire sauce

1 teaspoon garlic salt

1 teaspoon seasoned salt

½ teaspoon onion salt

1 pound butter, melted

In large bowl, toss together first 5 ingredients. Stir seasonings into melted butter and pour over dry mixture, stirring well to coat. Spread onto parchment-lined baking sheets and bake at 250 degrees for 2 hours, stirring every half hour. YIELD: 8 QUARTS.

Spiced Wassail

3 quarts apple cider

2 cinnamon sticks

½ teaspoon nutmeg

½ cup honey

⅓ cup lemon juice

2 teaspoons grated lemon peel

5 cups pineapple juice

3 whole oranges

Whole cloves

Bring cider and cinnamon sticks to a boil; reduce heat and simmer for 5 minutes. Add remaining ingredients, except oranges and cloves, and simmer 5 minutes longer, uncovered. Stud oranges with whole cloves and place in small baking pan with 2 tablespoons water. Bake at 325 degrees for 30 minutes. When ready to serve, float oranges in punch bowl with wassail. Remove cinnamon sticks or leave them to float with oranges. Wassail is best served warm. YIELD: 20 CUPS.

Spicy Guacamole

3 ripe avocados
1 ripe roma tomato, chopped
1 tablespoon dried minced onion
1 teaspoon lemon juice
2 tablespoons picante sauce or salsa

½ teaspoon salt
½ teaspoon garlic powder
Dash pepper
4 drops hot sauce

Peel and mash or cube avocado. Gently mix in remaining ingredients. Let stand for 15 minutes and serve at room temperature, or refrigerate and serve cold. YIELD: 6 SERVINGS.

Toasted Tortilla Chips with Mango Salsa

CHIPS:
1 dozen flour tortillas
Vegetable oil
Salt

SALSA:
2 ripe mangos, peeled and diced;
   or 1 (26 ounce) jar mango slices,
   diced
1 medium red bell pepper, diced

1 jalapeño pepper, seeded and diced
3 tablespoons chopped
   fresh cilantro
2 tablespoons chopped fresh mint
1 small red onion, chopped
2 tablespoons honey
1 tablespoon lime juice
½ teaspoon salt
¼ teaspoon ground red pepper

Brush top side of each tortilla with oil. Cut into 8 wedges and spread on parchment-lined baking sheet. Sprinkle with salt. Bake at 375 degrees for 10 to 15 minutes or until crispy brown. For salsa, mix together all ingredients, cover, and chill for at least 2 hours. YIELD: 4 TO 6 SERVINGS. (Double or triple ingredients depending on number of guests.)

Stuffed Mushrooms

4 or 5 slices bacon, fried crisp and crumbled
12 fresh sturdy mushroom caps, stems removed
12 (1 inch) cubes mozzarella cheese
Grated parmesan cheese

Divide bacon into each mushroom cap cavity. Place mozzarella cube in each cap. Place under oven broiler for about 5 minutes or until cheese is soft. Remove and sprinkle with parmesan. Serve hot. YIELD: 12 MUSHROOMS.

Teriyaki Chicken Wings

½ cup soy sauce
½ cup pineapple juice
2 tablespoons dried minced garlic
1 tablespoon ginger

½ teaspoon salt
½ teaspoon white pepper
2 dozen chicken wings
Pineapple chunks for garnish

Mix first 6 ingredients; add chicken wings and marinate in refrigerator for several hours. Remove from sauce and place on foil-lined baking sheet. Bake at 375 degrees for 30 to 40 minutes. Serve with pineapple chunks on toothpicks. YIELD: 24 WINGS.

Tomato Toddy

1 (46 ounce) can tomato juice
1 (46 ounce) bottle vegetable juice (such as V8)
¾ cup sugar
15 whole cloves
4 cinnamon sticks
1 teaspoon salt
3 cups water
¼ cup lemon juice
1 teaspoon celery salt
1 teaspoon paprika

Simmer all ingredients for about 15 minutes. Remove whole spices and serve hot. YIELD: 15 CUPS.

Zesty Salmon Pate

1 (8 ounce) package cream cheese, softened
2 tablespoons snipped parsley
2 teaspoons finely chopped green onion
1 teaspoon seasoned salt
¼ teaspoon garlic powder
1 teaspoon hot sauce
1 (8 ounce) can salmon, drained and flaked
Parsley stems or lemon slices for garnish
Variety of crackers

Combine first 7 ingredients until well mixed. Pour into 2-cup mold of any design and refrigerate for several hours. Unmold and add garnish. Serve with crackers. YIELD: 2 CUPS.

Index

Refreshing Beverages

Choco-Mint Cocoa..9

Cinnamon Cocoa...9

Cranberry Apple Sippers..9

Cranberry Spritzers...10

Down Under Christmas Smoothies..............................11

Eggnog..11

French Chocolate..11

Hot Chai...12

Hot Chocolate..12

Hot Spiced Tea..12

Mint-Chocolate Coffee Mix..13

Mulled Cider Mix..14

Peppermint Cocoa Mix...15

Peppermint Mocha Soda...15

Pineapple Frost..16

Pineapple-Orange Fizzes..16

Pumpkin Nog..17

Raspberry Lemonade...16

Rich "South of the Border" Hot Chocolate.................19

Spicy Grape Punch...20

Spicy Tea...20

Vanilla Ginger Latte 19

Yuletide Chocolate Lover's Coffee 18

Bountiful Breakfasts and Brunches

BREAKFAST

Apple Pancake Pie 23

Apple Pancakes 23

Bacon Gravy 24

Blueberry Coffee Cake 25

Blueberry Pancakes 25

Breakfast Casserole 26

Breakfast Pizza 26

Buttermilk Pancakes 27

Caramel Apple Grits 29

Cheesy Grits Casserole 29

Chorizo and Egg Burritos 28

Cinnamon Coffee Cake 30

Cinnamon Raisin French Toast 31

Cinnamon-Topped Oatmeal Muffins 32

Coffee Break Cake 30

Cornmeal Mush 33

Country Christmas Breakfast Casserole 33

Creamed Eggs and Biscuits 34

Crepes 35

Deluxe Grits 34

Doughnuts 36

Egg Fajitas 37

Eggs Benedict with Blender Hollandaise Sauce 38

Eggs Florentine 37

Eggs in the Hole 38

Energy Bars 41

German Oven Pancake 39

Ginger Pear Jam 44

Gingerbread Waffles 42

Glazed Breakfast Fruit 44

Grandma's Sausage Gravy and Country Biscuits 47

Granola 45

Holiday Breakfast Grits 48

Maple Syrup 48

Matchless Coconut Almond Granola 51

Oven-Baked Omelet 48

Overnight French Toast 46

Parfait Fruit Cups 52

Pear Breakfast Cake 52

Potato Pancakes (Latkes) 49

Sausage and Cheese Grits Casserole 50

South-of-the-Border Breakfast Casserole 53

Swedish Oven Pancakes 51

Waffles 54

Whole-Wheat Muffins 54

BRUNCH

Apple Cake 55

Apple Cream Scones 56

Apple Dumplings 57

Apple Ring 55

Apple Walnut Squares 57

Breakfast Sausage Bake 58

Butterscotch Coffee Cake 58

Christmas Braid 62

Christmas Wreath Coffee Cake 61

Date Rolls 60

Fruit Dip 61

Hot Peach Marlow 62

Norwegian Coffee Cake..59

Orange Date Bars..63

Raspberry Bars...65

Rhubarb Crunch...64

Spinach Mushroom Quiche...65

Tuna Cheese Crescent Squares..66

Tuna Quiche...66

Christmas Dinner, Including Main Dishes and Sides

MAIN DISHES

Baked Pork Chops and Apples..69

Chicken Diane...69

Chicken Orange...70

Cornish Hens with Basil-Walnut Sauce......................................71

Country Holiday Ham...75

Creamy Chicken and Rice with Thyme.......................................71

Festive Holiday Ham...75

Glazed Ham..72

Ham with Apple Relish..76

Herbed Cornish Hens..74

Holiday Ham Casserole...76

Home-Style Roast Beef..79

Home-Style Turkey..77

Honey Roast Ham...80

Huntington Chicken..80

Italian Turkey...79

Lasagna..83

Lemon-Herb Turkey Breast...84

Orange Duck...87

Oriental Charcoal-Broiled Roast...87

Pheasant with Wild Rice Stuffing...88

Roast Beef with Yorkshire Pudding 85

Roast Goose with Browned Potatoes 89

Rotisserie-Style Chicken 88

Savory Pork Roast 83

Sweet-and-Sour Chops 86

Traditional Christmas Turkey 84

Turkey Scaloppini 90

Veal in Wine with Mushrooms 81

Venison Roast 78

SIDES

Almond Rice 91

Auntie's Bean Salad 92

Candy Apple Salad 91

Cauliflower Salad 96

Champagne Salad 92

Chive Mashed Potatoes 95

Christmas Fruit Salad 93

Cinnamon Sweet Potatoes 94

Corn Bread Dressing 95

Cranberry Salad 99

Cranberry Waldorf Salad 99

Creamy Corn Casserole 97

English Pea Casserole 96

Evergreen Gelatin Salad 99

Farmhouse Potato Salad 98

French Rice 100

French-Style Green Beans 100

Fresh Cranberry Relish 100

Glazed Carrots 101

Green Peas with Celery and Onions 103

Kidney Bean Salad 103

Layered Broccoli-Cauliflower Salad 104

Make-Ahead Mashed Potatoes 102

Mandarin Orange Salad 103

Marinated Mushroom-Spinach Salad 105

Marinated Vegetable Salad 104

Mixed Vegetable Medley 111

Old-Fashioned Bread Stuffing 106

Old-Fashioned Mashed Potatoes 107

Orange–Sweet Potato Casserole 107

Oyster Corn Bread Dressing 108

Spinach-Stuffed Tomatoes 108

Stuffed Winter Squash 109

Sweet Potato Casserole 111

Willett's Broccoli-Rice Tradition 110

Wilted Spinach Salad 112

Zesty Carrots 112

Christmas Eve Celebrations

Bierock Casserole 115

Broiled Shrimp 115

Cheddar Chowder 116

Cheesy Broccoli Chowder 116

Corn Chowder 117

Cream of Zucchini Soup 118

Creamy Tomato Soup 124

Curried Butternut Squash Soup 119

Herb Potato Soup 119

Herbed Salmon Steaks 121

Hot Seafood Salad 120

Lamb Stew 120

Nana's Baked Beans 122

Peanut Butter Soup 123

Shrimp Newburg 123

Shrimp with Pasta 124

Cookies and Candy

COOKIES

Angel Cookies 127
Apricot Balls 128
Butterfinger Cookies 129
Buttermilk Cookies 127
Candy Cane Cookies 128
Chocolate Caramel Cookies 131
Chocolate Drop Cookies 130
Chocolate Holiday Cookies 132
Chocolate Snowballs 131
Christmas Bells 134
Christmas Hands 135
Christmas M&M Cookies 136
Christmas Tea Cookies 136
Cinnamon Nut Cookies 139
Cookies in a Jiffy 132
Cowboy Cookies 133
French Christmas Cookies 137
French Lace 140
Gingerbread Men 148
Grapefruit Sugar Cookies 138
Holiday Fruit Drops 140
Italian Christmas Cookies 143
Jam Thumbprints 142
Mrs. Santa's Cinnamon Cookies 144
Oatmeal Drop Cookies 145
Old-Fashioned Gingersnaps 147
Old-Fashioned Molasses Cookies 141

Old-Fashioned Preserve Thumbprints...135

Old-Fashioned Snickerdoodles...143

Orange-Iced Cranberry Cookies...144

Pecan Care Bears...148

Pecan Tassies...139

Peppermint Meringue Drops...149

Perfect Pumpkin Cookies...151

Plum Jam Cookies...147

Rosemary Crescents...150

Shortbread...146

CANDY

Almond Coconut Clusters...152

Banana Clusters...155

Bull's Eyes...153

Butterscotch Delights...152

Caramel Apples...154

Caramel Nut Cups...156

Caramel Popcorn...156

Cashew Brittle...159

Chocolate-Covered Cherries...157

Chocolate-Covered Strawberries...155

Chocolate-Dipped Dried Apricots...158

Chocolate-Dipped Candy Canes...159

Chocolate-Dipped Pretzels...162

Chocolate Haystacks...160

Chocolate Truffles...161

Christmas Crunchies...163

Christmas Mints...160

Crispy Cereal Chocolate Drops...168

Delicious Date Balls...169

Divinity Fudge...163

Holiday Chocolate Fudge...167

Peanut Brittle 164

Peanut Butter Bark 164

Peanut Butter Kisses 168

Pecan Pralines 172

Rock Candy 170

Toffee 171

Turtles 171

Festive Breads

Apple Bread 185

Banana Bread 177

Butter Pecan Bread 175

Cheese Biscuits 178

Christmas Morning Blueberry Biscuits 188

Christmas Morning Cinnamon Rolls 179

Christmas Pound Cake 179

Christmas Sweet Bread 176

Cinnamon Swirl Bread 189

Cranberry Bread 190

Date Bread 175

Easy Cinnamon Rolls 181

Em's Rusks 176

Gingerbread 182

Granny's Corn Bread 183

Holiday Muffins 183

Hominy Bread 184

Honey Apple Raisin Nut Bread 184

Honey Wheat Bread 187

Mayonnaise Biscuits 188

Monkey Bread 187

Nana's Banana Bread 191

Oatmeal Muffins 191

Parmesan Breadsticks 180

Pumpkin Bread 193

Pumpkin Corn Bread 192

Pumpkin Muffins 186

South African Overnight Bread 192

Sweet Potato Biscuits 180

Zucchini Bread 194

Merrymaking: Party Dishes to Feed a Crowd

Apple-Orange Punch 197

Bacon-Wrapped Water Chestnuts 199

Broccoli Squares 197

Christmas Coffee Punch 197

Christmas Tradition Gyozas 200

Cocktail Meatballs 203

Corn and Bacon Dip 198

Cranberry Pecan Spread 198

Cream Cheese Pinwheels 198

Dressed Eggs 201

Double Lime Punch 201

Four-Cheese Ball 204

Fruit Dip 202

Golden Christmas Punch 202

Holiday Salsa 208

Jalapeño Dill Dip 205

Milk Punch 205

Olive Crescents 205

Party Nibbles 209

Party Pecans 207

Party Punch Ring 206

Pita Poppers 206

Spiced Wassail 209

Spicy Guacamole 210

Stuffed Mushrooms 211

Teriyaki Chicken Wings 212

Toasted Tortilla Chips with Mango Salsa 210

Tomato Toddy 213

Zesty Salmon Pate 213